The Democratic Corporation

Russell L. Ackoff

The Democratic Corporation

**A Radical Prescription
for Recreating Corporate America
and Rediscovering Success**

New York   Oxford
OXFORD UNIVERSITY PRESS
1994

Oxford University Press

Oxford   New York   Toronto
Delhi   Bombay   Calcutta   Madras   Karachi
Kuala Lumpur   Singapore   Hong Kong   Tokyo
Nairobi   Dar es Salaam   Cape Town
Melbourne   Auckland   Madrid

and associated companies in
Berlin   Ibadan

Copyright © 1994 by Oxford University Press, Inc.

Published by Oxford University Press, Inc.
200 Madison Avenue, New York, New York 10016

Oxford is a registered trademark of Oxford University Press

Library of Congress Cataloging-in-Publication Data
Ackoff, Russell Lincoln, 1919–
The democratic corporation : a radical prescription
for recreating corporate America
and rediscovering success /
Russell L. Ackoff. p.   cm.
Includes bibliographical references and index.
ISBN 0-19-508727-5
1. Industrial management.   I. Title.
HC38.A27   1994
658—dc20   93-35403

9 8 7 6 5 4 3 2 1

Printed in the United States of America
on acid-free paper

To my very good friend
Leon Pritzker
who has been telling me
what's wrong since 1946—
and
has almost always been right.

Preface

The deterioration of the American economy in general and many American enterprises in particular is now widely recognized and discussed. More frequently than not, this situation is approached with what appears to be a tendency to oversimplify the problem—hence its solution. Most of those who manage our society and enterprises within it are panacea-prone. Rather than meditate, they recite such mantras as *total quality management, continuous improvement, and right-sizing.*

> "Right-sizing"—eliminating unnecessary infrastructure and reducing management layers—is becoming the most common tactic of most corporations. . . . In most cases, right-sizing isn't part of a thoughtful strategy to redesign the whole corporate management structure and culture. Instead, it's an almost panicked reaction to pressures and problems, administered with the sheeplike justification that everyone else is doing the same thing. [Emshoff, p. x]

In addition, managers are preoccupied with *core competence, process engineering, strategic alliances,* and *competitive strategies;* and not too long ago there was a rush to practice *value analysis, maximizing shareholder value,* and *sensitivity training,* among many other things.

The deterioration of the American economy and its enterprises is not *a* problem but a complex system of interrelated problems. I call such systems messes. A mess cannot be handled effectively by breaking it down into its constituent parts and solving each part separately. As we will see, the way problems and their solutions interact is much more important than how they act independently of each other. The current mess is so deeply rooted in our society that nothing short of a radical transformation of our economy and its institutions will reverse their deteriorating trend.

This book is an attempt to chart a way out of our current mess, an effort to mobilize change by developing an understanding of the mess we are in (Part I) and what can be done about it (Part II). I believe strongly that the ideas advocated in this book can change failure to success. But there may be other ways that will work as well. The important thing is to begin the process of reforming organizations now, and I hope these ideas will stimulate that beginning.

As Peter Drucker (1968), Alvin Toffler (1971), Donald Schon (1971), and John Naisbitt (1982), among many others, have shown, the changes we are experiencing are profound. Therefore, they require profound changes if they are to be converted from threats to opportunities.

> Unprecedented social, political, and technological changes have occurred during this century. More profound changes lie ahead. To make the decisions that will be required, we must understand the nature of change itself—its causes and effects—its dangers and possibilities. How to create a more desirable and humane future is of urgent and vital concern. [Cooper-Hewitt Museum, *The Phenomenon of Change* (1984), cover]

In Chapter 1 I show how the concept of an enterprise has evolved since the Renaissance—from its being thought of first as a machine, then as an organism, and now as a social system. I argue that this evolution mirrors that of the worldview which prevailed in the West, its concept of the nature of reality. The central role of the concept "system" in this story is critical, and therefore its meaning and its relevance to the emerging concept of an enterprise are explored in depth.

In Chapter 2 I explore three different views of an enterprise that are revealed by looking at it sociosystemically: from the inside out, from the outside in, and from the inside in. These views are based on recognition of the importance to an enterprise of all its stakeholders—those who are directly affected by what it does. In addition, I consider the appropriate objective of an enterprise conceptualized as a social system— *development*—and how it differs from growth. Then I explore the "dimensions" of development and its counterpart, effectiveness: science, economics, ethics, and aesthetics.

In Chapter 3 I argue for a new approach to the way we pursue the elusive matter of quality. The current preoccupation with quality derives from a transformation of focus from growth and its measure, standard of living, to development and its measure, quality of life. I explore the meaning of quality of life in general, and quality of work life in particular, and show the futility of efforts to measure them. However, I also show that the need to do so can be removed by a participative activity I call "idealized design." I diagnose the frequent failure of quality-of-work-life programs and prescribe corrective actions. Then I discuss TQM's preoccupation with the quality of products and services from the consumer's point of view. First, I consider how one can determine what consumers actually want, which is by no means easy to do. Then the shortcomings of continuous improvement from a systemic point of view are revealed, and an antidote—planning backward from an ideal—is described.

In chapters 4 through 6 I present three compatible designs of enterprises that can be used separately or in combination to transform them from ones that may have been well equipped to survive in an era that is rapidly drawing to a close, to an enterprise well equipped to thrive, let alone survive, in the emerging era. The emerging era goes under a variety of names, including the Information Age, the Era of the Global Economy, the Age of Discontinuity, and the Systems Age.

In Chapter 4 I describe the design of a democratic hierarchy, a circular organization. In this type of organization all members can participate directly or indirectly in decisions that affect them, and there is no ultimate authority. I show how such an organization enables people to do as well as they know how, to develop, and to have fun, and how these facilitate meeting a systemic requirement, the management of interactions.

In Chapter 5 I consider how the centrally planned and centrally controlled (sovietlike) economies of most enterprises can be converted into market economies, and what the advantages are of doing so. It eliminates the chance of an organization becoming hopelessly noncompetitive and the need for benchmarking; it reveals what activities should be integrated and which should not, and how to coordinate semiautonomous activities so that the enterprise as a whole adds value to each of its parts.

In Chapter 6 I ask why such frequent reorganization of enterprises as they currently undergo are necessary, and I find the reasons in the way they divide labor and in changes that occur in their internal and external environments. Then I show a multidimensional organization design that makes continuous adaptation to change possible without reorganizing.

Finally, in the Epilogue I deal with this question: Since the ideas set forth in this book have been successfully applied in a number of enterprises and this has been public information for some time, why haven't they been more widely adopted? Perhaps the most important reason lies in management miseducation. I consider a number of erroneous ideas about management, enterprises, and their environments that such education propagates. I identify its principal effects as providing those who survive it with a vocabulary that enables them to talk authoritatively about subjects they do not understand, and inculcating them with principles that have demonstrated their ability to withstand any amount of disconfirming evidence. However, it does provide them with a ticket of admission to a career in which they can either preserve the currently prevailing state of ignorance or initiate the kinds of transformations in their enterprises that can elevate them to new levels of service to their stakeholders and society.

The difficulty in business education is not lack of relevant knowledge. Most of the knowledge used by the Japanese to gain ascendancy in the world's economy is available here, in the West. However, the Japanese are using more of what the West knows than the West is, and what both use they use better than the West does. Little wonder, then, that the Japanese are willing to open their doors and let us look in. They don't believe we have the ability to use what we know as well as they do. To a large extent they attribute this to the complacency of Western managers whose belief in business cycles provides them with false assurance that what comes down must eventually go up again, and the nature of business-school "education" in the West. For example, *Fortune* (1986) reported Asa Jonishi, director of Japan's Kyocera Corporation, as saying, "Theories taught in management schools are often useless when applied to practical business. That is why we think the Harvard Business School is a remarkable school but may be more of a detriment to the U.S. economy" (p. 14).

Western managers generally believe their poor performance in the global marketplace is due to factors that are out of their control. This belief provides them with a basis for rationalizing their disinclination to make fundamental changes. Their high personal standards of living apply no pressure on them to reconsider this belief. Western managers treat change as a threat; the Japanese treat it as an opportunity. Western managers are preoccupied with avoiding *errors of commission,* doing something that does not have to be done; Japanese managers are preoccupied with *errors of omission*, failing to do something that should be done. Western managers are willing to settle for survival, doing well enough; the Japanese are dissatisfied with less than "thrival," doing as well as possible.

Despite the fact that the Japanese are using more of what the West knows than the West is, there is a great deal that is known in the West that neither it nor the Japanese are using. Surpassing the Japanese is possible, but not by imitating them. Imitators seldom catch up to those they imitate. The Japanese did not surpass the West by imitating it but by leapfrogging over it.

There are not enough institutional and organizational leaders in America who understand the prevailing mess, let alone know how to deal with it. Our only hope for stemming the retreating tide is to stimulate enough of the right kind of leadership by confronting it with the right kind of ideas, ideas that mobilize our human resources into concerted, constructive action. This hope may not provide much ground for optimism, but it is the only hope we have.

Philadelphia   R. L. A.
October 1993

Contents

The Democratic Corporation

The Dopaminergic Connection

Part *I*

Background

This part attempts to develop understanding of the prevailing mess. It shows how the concept of an enterprise emerged during the Industrial Revolution, and how it has changed since then. The currently emerging concept of an enterprise is one that provides a completely new view of a corporation and its responsibilities to society and its internal and external stakeholders. It is a concept that has to be grasped by most of those who manage our institutions and organizations because it makes it possible for them to deal effectively with the system of problems they now face.

Chapter *1*

The Emerging Concept of an Enterprise

In this chapter I consider how and why the concept of an enterprise has evolved since the Renaissance—from the enterprise conceptualized as a machine, then as an organism, and now as a social system. Then I consider the implications of looking at an enterprise as a *system*, what doing so should mean to management and the way work is organized. In this chapter and in Chapter 2 I will consider the implication of looking at enterprises as *social* systems.

The way we view an enterprise is affected by our worldview. This view consists of the most fundamental assumptions we make about the nature of reality and how we can come to know and understand it. Currently in the West, the prevailing view of the world is greatly influenced by two characteristics of our environment: its rate of change and its increasing complexity.

At least since 1971, when Alvin Toffler published *Future Shock*, it has been obvious to most of us who live in the West that we are subject to an increasing rate of change and increasing complexity. The complexity of our environment increases with increases in the number of interactions we must take into account when making decisions. Because of recent developments in communication and transportation, many more enterprises, institutions, and societies are interacting than ever did in the past. For this reason we now refer to the economy in which we operate as *global*.

An environment that is simultaneously undergoing an accelerating rate of change and becoming more complex is said to be *turbulent* (Emery and Trist, 1965). Turbulence consists of such changes as are virtually impossible to predict (Coffey, 1983, and Newman, 1980). Paul Valery (1989) used a term other than turbulence to describe the current state of affairs and its principal consequence:

> This state of things, which I call "chaotic," is the combined result of the works and the accumulated labor of men. Of course it points to some kind of future, but one that is absolutely impossible for us to imagine; and among many other innovations, *this* is one of the greatest. We can no longer deduce from what we know any notion of the future to which we can give the slightest credence. [pp. 130-131]

Therefore, the challenge facing managers of enterprises is how to survive, let alone thrive, in an increasingly turbulent environment and how to prepare for a future that cannot be predicted accurately.

Some, like Robert W. Lucky (1990), find this challenge difficult to face because it is so difficult to define:

> Somewhere out there, things are going on. Inventions are being made, concepts are being formulated, theorems are being proved, methodologies and processes are being conceived, markets are rising and falling, and styles are being shaped. But these things take place in a cacophony of false starts. Technology is like an orchestra tuning up. If you listen hard, you can hear little

fragments of recognizable pieces. But if your attention lapses, you hear nothing but noise.

If you find out what is going on, please let me know. I am desperate. [p. 6]

Lucky is not alone. Nevertheless, he did formulate succinctly the question to which this chapter is devoted: What is going on?

When our environment changes, the way we perceive and conceptualize that environment and the enterprises it contains also tends to change. Moreover, objective changes in enterprises and their environments and subjective changes in the way we perceive and conceptualize them affect each other. As James Ogilvy (1989) observed about Thomas Kuhn (1970) and others, "each . . . sees the violence and turbulence of those periods of disequilibrium when one world and its corresponding worldview gives way to another" (p. 8). What we experience affects the way we think, and what we think affects what we experience. Objectivity and subjectivity are like the two sides of a coin: They can be seen and discussed separately, but they cannot be separated. Their interaction is clearly revealed in the evolution of the way we have conceptualized enterprises.

The Mechanistic View of the World

When the Industrial Revolution began in the West, the prevailing worldview was Newtonian. Newton thought of the world as a hermetically sealed clock, a mechanism that operated with a regularity dictated by its internal structure and the causal laws of nature, laws he believed he had formulated. Therefore he viewed the world as a closed, self-contained, mechanical system, one that had no environment.

In general, what occurs in the world was thought to be understandable without reference to the environments in which they occur. This is reflected in the fact that most physical laws of that period described what things would do, or what events would occur, in the *absence* of an environment. For example, the Law of Freely Falling Bodies reveals the distance a body *would* fall in a specified amount of time *in a vacuum*. A vacuum is the absence of an environment. Furthermore, most research was conducted in laboratories, places deliberately constructed to eliminate the effect of the environment on the study of the effect of one variable on another.

Newton also believed that the world was a machine that God had created to do his work, to serve his purposes. This belief was shared by most others in the Western world regardless of their religious differences. From pulpits of every sect people were told that they were here to do God's will. James Joyce's (1947) fictional Father Arnall put it very clearly: "And remember, my dear boys, that we have been sent into the world for one thing and for one thing alone: to do God's holy will and to save our immortal souls. All else is worthless (p. 362)." Those who transmitted such messages claimed to have received them from God by revelation.

Most people in the West also believed the claim made in Genesis that people had been created in the image of God. (This claim was not surprising, considering its source.) These two beliefs—that the world was a machine created by God to do his work, and that people had been created in his image— formed the premises of a syllogism that concluded with: *Humans, like God, should create machines to do their work*. This belief was a source of the Industrial Revolution.

The Industrial Revolution

The Industrial Revolution began in England in the eighteenth century and then spread to other parts of the world. It did not reach the United States until about a century later because this country was largely occupied with pushing back its frontiers, settling the land, and developing the infrastructure—particularly transportation and communication—required to support industrialization. The revolution consisted of the replacement of people by machines as sources of energy. It was not until the eighteenth century that the amount and kind of technology required for large-scale industrialization became available.

Work was thought of as the application of energy to matter so as to change its properties. For example, such activities as moving an object, burning coal, and shaping steel were considered to be work. Machines were taken to be objects that could be used to apply energy to matter. All things were thought to be reducible to indivisible particles of matter, atoms. Similarly, machines were thought to be reducible to three elementary machines: the wheel and axle, the lever arm, and the inclined plane. By means of what came to be known as "work study," work was similarly reduced by analysis to ultimately simple tasks. The simpler the tasks, the easier they were to mechanize. Machines were then developed to perform as many of these elementary tasks as were technologically and economically feasible. People were assigned to those that were not. Then people and machines were organized into sequences and networks of tasks, the apotheosis of which was mass production and the assembly line.

Mechanization affected the nature of the tasks left for people to perform. Workers no longer did all the things necessary to produce a product; rather, they repeatedly performed simple operations that were a very small part of the production process. (This was the focus of Charlie Chaplin's satire in his film *Modern Times.*) Consequently, the more machines were used as substitutes for people, the more people at work were made to behave like machines. Mechanization led to the dehumanization of work done by people. This was the irony of the Industrial Revolution.

It is not surprising that a society that thought of the world as a machine also came to think of the enterprises created by the Industrial Revolution as machines and the people who worked in them as replaceable machine parts.

The Enterprise as a Machine

Business enterprises were initially thought of as machines created by their gods, their owners, to do their work. Enterprises, conceptualized as machines, like all machines, were attributed with no purpose of their own, but were believed to have the function of serving their owners' purposes. Their principal purpose was to obtain an adequate return on their investment of time, money, and effort. This required that enterprises make a profit. Making a profit came to be thought of as the *only* legitimate function of an enterprise. This belief is still held by many, as reflected in the writing of Milton Friedman (1970): "[T]here is one and only one social responsibility of business—to use its resources and engage in activities designed to increase its profits so long as it stays within the rules of the game . . ." (p. 125). The same point of view was expressed more recently by Rappaport (1986). It is far from dead.

Owners of early enterprises were present and powerful; they ran their businesses with virtually no constraints. They were godlike in the small worlds they had created. Employees were known to be human, of course, but their personal interests and purposes were taken to be irrelevant to their employers. Workers were retained only as long as they were ready, willing, and able to do what the owners wanted. When they no longer were, like replaceable machine parts, they were discarded and replaced by others who were compliant and usable. This was even true of managers: E. E. Jennings (1971), writing of the life of managers during this period, observed: "Family life became just another *cog in the corporate machine* (p. 29; italics mine).

In the early days of industrialization the work done by most employees required little or no skill, and unskilled labor was plentiful. In general, the members of the workforce had little education and therefore relatively low levels of aspiration. Many were immigrants who had only a very limited knowledge of English. They aspired more for their children than for themselves. For most workers, employment was necessary for survival. Unemployment often resulted in economic destitution. There was no Social Security, no unemployment insurance or welfare, and the average compensation of workers was not large enough to enable them to insure themselves against unemployment. Little wonder, then, that many were willing to work under almost any conditions, and they did.

The Decline of the Mechanistic View of an Enterprise

The conception of an enterprise as a machine started to become less tenable in the last few decades of the nineteenth century. By the end of World War I, the mechanistic conception was largely replaced by one that was *biological;* enterprises were increasingly thought of as *organisms* rather than as machines.

There were a number of reasons for this transformation. Both the educational level of workers and their levels of aspiration had increased. Government began to regulate working conditions, thereby reducing the power of the owners and protecting at least the biological welfare (health and safety) of members of the workforce. Unions emerged and began to improve the conditions of work, work itself, compensation for it, and job security.

However, the most important reason for the transition from the mechanistic to the organismic conception of enterprises was the fact that their owners could not exploit all the opportunities for growth of their enterprises even if all their profits were reinvested in their growth. In addition, the increased technology of production required increased amounts of investment in facilities and equipment. "In order to buy the capital equipment necessary for new and expanded operations, corporations have traditionally gone to the investing public for funds" (Mouzelis, 1974, p. 184). Therefore, to unleash growth and productivity, many owners had to raise additional capital by selling stock. This required most of them to relinquish at least some control over the enterprises they had created. The survival and growth rates of those enterprises that raised investment capital by "going public" were much greater than of those whose owners elected to retain control and constrain growth.

When an enterprise went public, its god disappeared. Stockholders were numerous, dispersed, anonymous to, and unreachable by members of the workforce. Some of the larger corporations acquired more than a million shareholders; one, AT&T, acquired over three million. Therefore, ownership became an abstraction, owners a spirit. How was communication with this spirit to be obtained? There was a precedent: Nineteen hundred years earlier, a Western God had disappeared and become an abstract spirit with whom ordinary men could not communicate directly. An institution and a profession—the church and its clergy—were created to bridge the gap. Similarly, as the nineteenth century drew to a close, management (the church) and managers (the clergy) were created to control enterprises in the alleged interests of their owners, and to discern and communicate their will to the employees. Managers came to know the shareholders' will in the same way the clergy claimed to know the will of God, by revelation.

The principal effect of the dispersion of "ownership" was to give effective control of enterprises to their managers. James Burnham (1941) referred to this as a "managerial revolution." He argued that enterprises were now run by managers primarily for their own benefit, not the owners'. Profit came to be thought of as a means, not an end. Like oxygen for a human being, profit was thought of as a means necessary for the *survival and growth* of the enterprise, not the reason for it. At the turn of the century, the American humorist Ambrose Bierce (1967) caught the spirit of this change of perspective in his definition of money: "A blessing that is of no advantage to us excepting when we part with it" (p. 226).

In the 1960s a very large and very successful corporation in the United States (which does not want its identity revealed for reasons that will be obvious) conducted a study to explain the decisions of its executives using profit maximization as the principal corporate objective. This study concluded that either the executives were incompetent or that profit maximization was not the corporation's principal objective. Those who conducted the study then asked: What objective would retrospectively have maximized the rationality of the decisions the executives had made? One objective was found that made almost all executive decisions "rational": maximization of the standard of living and quality of work life of those executives who made the decisions, not shareholder value. Providing shareholders with adequate returns had been treated as a *requirement for survival*, not an objective. Survival is a biological concept, not mechanical.

The Enterprise as an Organism

Like all biological entities, the enterprise came to be considered as having survival as a purpose of its own. Growth was believed to be essential for it. The opposite of growth—contraction—was taken to be slow death. (A detailed and very complete discussion of "organicism" can be found in Stark, 1963.)

Publicly owned enterprises came to be called "corporations." This word derives from the Latin word *corpus*, meaning "body" (organisms have bodies, machines do not). Moreover, in the eyes of the law, the corporation was endowed with the status of a biological individual. In 1886 the U.S. Supreme Court ruled for the first time that a corporation should be

construed as a person (Mouzelis, 1974, p. 183). Biological met-
aphors invaded organizational thinking. The chief executive
came to be called "the head" of the organization (organisms
have heads, machines do not). Other biological concepts came
to be applied to enterprises—for example, viable, healthy,
sick, paralyzed, and energetic. Such concepts are still commonly used. For example, not very long ago Stafford Beer
wrote books titled *The Brain of the Firm* (1972) and *The Heart of
the Enterprise* (1979).

Because of continuing advances in mechanization, the
skills required of workers continued to increase. Those who
had the required skills were not as plentiful as those who
didn't. The cost of replacing skilled workers was not neg-
ligible—a significant amount of costly training was frequently
involved. As a result, they came to be treated more like
difficult-to-replace organs than easily replaceable machine
parts. The health and safety of employees received increasing
attention not only from unions but also from government.
However relevant the functions of workers were taken to be,
their interests and purposes were still not considered to be an
appropriate concern of their employers.

The expansion of Social Security and increases of personal
savings (resulting from increased compensation for work) reduced the connection between economic destitution and unemployment. Furthermore, unions negotiated increased job
security. These developments encouraged dissatisfied employees to protest against what they considered to be unfair
labor practices and bad working conditions. Management and
labor came to see themselves as irrevocably opposed to the
other, much as many philosophers took mind and body to be.

The Decline of the Organismic View of an Enterprise

The biological view of the enterprise still prevails, but it has
eroded significantly since World War II. At that time, a major

portion of the workforce was drafted into military service. Nevertheless, demands for production were very great. Young people, the elderly, and especially women were drawn into the workforce. (Recall Rosie the Riveter and Tillie the Toiler.) These replacements for workers who had been drafted into the military were motivated more by patriotism than by the need for income. Many were supported by allowances given to dependents of servicemen. Managers who wanted high productivity from members of this patriotically driven workforce could not obtain it by treating them as replaceable machine parts or even as functioning but purposeless organs; they had to be treated as human beings with purposes of their own.

Because of accelerated mechanization and automation after the war, the skills and education required of the workforce increased dramatically. More and more time and money were invested in the education and training of employees at all levels, including managers. To obtain a return on this investment, employees had to be used more productively and retained for longer periods of time. This could not be done by treating those who had returned to the workforce from military services as they had been treated in the military. Autocracy and strict discipline had become repugnant to them.

E. E. Jennings (1971) wrote about the change in attitudes toward work of managers:

> Then came World War II . . . and innovation was needed at all levels; no one person could possibly know enough to maintain corporate viability. Corporations began placing their chips on young men not yet mesmerized by the loyalty ethic. . . . Young executives grew self-confident that they could manage their own careers. . . . When they saw upward mobility arrested, they opted for opportunities elsewhere. . . . The most mobile had the best chance to achieve and acquire experience; mobility bred competency that in turn bred mobility. Rapid executive turnover became a fact of life. [p. 29]

Ex-GIs returning to civilian work wanted to be treated as unique individuals with needs and desires of their own. This was reflected in the permissive way they raised their children. As a result, the post-World War II "baby boomers" were even less inclined than their parents to tolerate authoritarian management. Most members of the permissive "Spock" generation had not experienced a depression, and therefore economic destitution was an abstraction to them, but job mobility was concrete and real. Furthermore, they did not attribute as much importance to material possessions as their parents had. They did not adopt the Protestant work ethic that characterized preceding generations, and they did not consider work to be an inherently good thing. Rather, they thought of work as a necessary evil. Recall the hippies of the 1960s and '70s.

The members of the permissive generation who went to work (and most of them eventually did) expected their interests to be taken into account by their employing organizations. Many managements failed to do so. As a result, many people were alienated from work and their employing organizations. According to *Work in America,* a report submitted to the U.S. secretary of health, education, and welfare in 1973:

> [S]ignificant numbers of American workers are dissatisfied with the quality of their working lives. Dull, repetitive, seemingly meaningless tasks, offering little challenge or autonomy, are causing discontent among workers at all occupational levels. This is not so much because work itself had greatly changed; indeed, one of the main problems is that work has not changed fast enough to keep up with the widespread changes in worker attitudes, aspirations, and values. A general increase in their educational and economic status has placed many American workers in a position where having an interesting job is now as important as a job that pays well. Pay is still important: it must support an "adequate" standard of living and be perceivable as equitable—but high pay alone will not lead to job (or life) satisfaction. [pp. xv–xvi]

Protest groups, outside as well as inside corporations, proliferated. Consumerists and environmentalists felt that they were being adversely affected by organizations of which they were not a part, or societies of which they were a part. These groups held corporations responsible for their allegedly harmful effects on society, its members, and the environment. This contributed to bringing about a transformation in the way people thought of an enterprise; they began to think of it as a social system.

The Enterprise as a Social System

Because of internally and externally applied pressures, corporate managers became aware of the need to take into account the concerns, interests, and objectives of the people who were part of the systems they managed and the larger systems that contained them—for example, society—and other systems that were parts of the same containing systems. In addition, these managers obviously had to be concerned with the purposes of the organizations they managed. This preoccupation with the purposes of parts and containing wholes made it increasingly difficult for managers to think of their organizations as either mechanical or biological systems. They began to think of them as *social systems,* systems in which people individually and collectively played the major roles.

This social systemic point of view contrasts sharply with Milton Friedman's:

> Executives insist that they have duties beyond maximizing value for shareholders. "We have 40,000 employees and 1.3 million representatives around the world," says Hicks B. Waldron, chairman of Avon Products, Inc. "We have a number of suppliers, institutions, customers, communities. None of them have the democratic freedom as shareholders do to buy or sell their shares. They have much deeper and much more important stakes

in our company than our shareholders." [Hoerr and Collingwood, 1987, p. 103]

Social systems are systems that have purposes of their own,
are made up of parts that have purposes of their own, and are
parts of larger systems that also have purposes of their own,
and these larger containing systems include other systems that
have purposes of their own. All these purposes came to be
recognized as relevant by those who managed enterprises.

The Post- or Second Industrial Revolution

Just as mechanistic thinking was accompanied by the Industrial Revolution, social systemic thinking has been accompanied by what has alternatively been called the Post- or
Second Industrial Revolution, but also the Information/
Knowledge Revolution and the Systems Revolution. The First
and Second industrial revolutions differ significantly.

In the nineteenth century, scientists and engineers began
to develop a variety of instruments for measuring the characteristics of electricity—for example, ammeters, voltmeters, and
ohmmeters. Strictly speaking, these instruments are not machines because they are not used to apply energy to matter so as
to transform that matter. Therefore, these instruments did not
do work; *they generated data*. Data are symbols that represent
the properties of objects or events. The generation of data,
when carried out by a human being, is called *observation*.
Therefore, in the middle of the past century, development of
the technology of observation began to accelerate.

Shortly thereafter, the sequence—telegraph, telephone,
wireless, radio, and television—was initiated. These devices
were not machines either, because they, too, were not involved
in work. What they did was *transmit symbols*. When a human
being does this it is called *communication*.

Almost a hundred years later, just before the middle of this century, the electronic computer was developed, a device that *manipulated symbols logically*. It, too, did no work. John Dewey (1938) called the logical manipulation of symbols *thinking*.

In about the middle of this century some scientists and engineers—stimulated in part by the philosopher Suzanne Langer (1948)—began to recognize that these three new technologies had a common characteristic: They all dealt with *symbols*. Then, in the spirit of systems thinking, they asked what the result would be of putting them together. They found that a system that generates data, transmits them from one entity to another, and can process them, thereby converting them into information and knowledge, would be a *mindlike* system. A technology had been developed to replace the minds of people in some instances. (The First Industrial Revolution replaced the *muscle* of man in some tasks in which muscle was required.) The replacement of mind by the new artifact was given the name *automation* by John Diebold (1952). Automation is to systems thinking what machines are to mechanistic thinking.

In the 1940s and '50s, when automation was increasingly applied, many began to worry that it would make people in general, and managers in particular, obsolete. If machines could replace people's minds as well as their muscles, what would ultimately be left for people to do? This concern was based on the incorrect assumption that there is a finite number of problems to which the human mind can be applied. Therefore, as the computer and automation took over more and more of these, they would decrease the role of and the need for human intervention.

The problems that can confront human minds are unlimited. No matter how many are solved, an infinite number will always remain to be solved. Every solution to a problem generates several new problems, and the new ones are generally more challenging than the one from which they sprang. Therefore, although automation reduces some of the problems that have to be considered by people, it increases the number and complexity of the problems that require their consideration. Witness the fact that although all the scientific problems formulated during the Renaissance have since been solved, the number and complexity of problems left for science to solve have increased continuously since then. It may well be that the progress of science is better measured by increases in the number and difficulty of the problems it faces than by the number of solutions it has obtained.

The Nature of Systems

Social systemic thinking requires fundamental changes in the way work is designed and organized and in the way the resulting organizations are managed. To know what changes are required and to understand why they are required, in turn requires an understanding of the nature of *systems* generally and the nature of *social* systems in particular. It was not until after World War II, when the shift from organismic to social-systemic thinking began to take place, that the "system" became a focal concept not only in organizational and managerial thinking but also in science, philosophy, and public affairs (Ackoff, 1981, ch. 1).

A system is a whole that contains two or more parts that satisfy the following five conditions.

1. The whole has one or more defining functions.

For example, a defining function of an automobile is to transport people on land. One of the defining functions of an enterprise is to produce and distribute wealth. The defining function of a corporate brewer is to produce, distribute, and market beer. Note that the fact that a system has a function implies its being a part of a larger system, its function being the role it plays in that larger system.

2. Each part in the set can affect the behavior or properties of the whole.

For example, the behavior of such parts of the human body as the heart, lungs, stomach, brain, and lungs can affect the performance and properties of the whole. On the other hand, the (vermiform) *appendix*, which is not known to have any effect on the whole, is not a part of the system but an *add-on* or *attachment* to it, as its name implies. (If the appendix is ever found to have an effect on the body's behavior or properties, its name will have to be changed.) The manuals, maps, and tools usually found in the glove compartment of a car are examples of appendices rather than parts of a car. Each phase of the brewing process—for example, malting, fermenting, pasteurizing or filtering, and packaging—affects the properties of the final product, and these properties affect the ability of the company to market its beer.

3. There is a subset of parts that is sufficient in one or more environments for carrying out the defining function of the whole; each of these parts is separately necessary but insufficient for carrying out this defining function.

These parts are *essential* to the system; without any one of them the system cannot carry out its defining function. An automobile's engine, fuel injector, steering wheel, and battery are essential for it—without them the automobile cannot transport people.

Most systems also contain nonessential parts that affect its functioning but not its essential function. An automobile's radio, ashtray, floor mats, and clock are nonessential, but they do affect automobile users in other ways—for example, by entertaining them.

A corporation is a system some of whose parts are essential—for example, finance, purchasing, production, and marketing—and some of which may not be—for example, public and employee relations. A corporation may also have appendices, such as a corporate foundation or a tenant in its building. Note that suppliers, wholesalers, retailers, and customers who are parts of a corporation's environment may also be essential to it. A system that requires certain environmental conditions to carry out its defining function is an *open* system. This is why the set of parts that form an open system cannot be sufficient for its performing its function in *every* environment. A system that could carry out its function in every environment would be completely independent of its environment and, therefore, be *closed*.

The environment of a system consists of those things that can affect the properties and performance of that system but over which it has no control. That part of its environment that can be influenced though not controlled is said to be *transactional*. Consumers and suppliers, for example, are part of a corporation's transactional environment. That part of a system's environment that can neither be influenced nor controlled is said to be *contextual*—for example, the weather and other natural events such as floods and earthquakes, and at least some competitive behavior.

4. The way that the behavior or properties of each part of a system affects its behavior or properties depends on the behavior or properties of at least one other part of the system.

Put another way, no part of a system has an independent effect on the system of which it is a part. For example, the way the heart affects the body depends on what the lungs are doing, and the way the lungs affect the body depends on what the heart, brain, and other parts are doing. The way a manufacturing department affects a corporation's performance depends on the behavior of its marketing department. The behavior and properties of the marketing department are affected by the behavior and properties of the production and engineering departments, and so on.

The parts of a system necessarily interact, either directly or indirectly. Therefore, a collection of automobiles, even if owned by one person, does not constitute a system because the automobiles do not interact. On the other hand, the two speakers of a stereo radio and the tuner and amplifier are parts of a system because they interact to produce a quality of sound that neither can produce alone.

> 5. The effect of any subset of parts on the system as a whole depends on the behavior of at least one other subset.

Like the individual parts of a system, no subsets of the parts of a system has an independent effect on it. For example, the effect of the metabolic subsystem on the human body depends on the behavior of the nervous subsystem, and the effect of the nervous subsystem depends on the behavior of the motor subsystem, and so on.

If the parts of a corporation do not interact, they form an aggregation, not a system. Many holding companies and conglomerates are aggregations, not systems; the only thing their parts have in common is their ownership. They do not interact.

Summarizing and oversimplifying, *a system is a whole that cannot be divided into independent parts.* This hardly seems revolutionary, but its implications are. Consider some of those that relate to organization and management, hence to corporations.

Part-Part Interactions

The performance of a system obviously depends on the performance of its parts, but an important, if not the most important, aspect of a part's performance is how it interacts with other parts to affect the performance of the whole. How part of a system performs when considered independently of the system of which it is a part is irrelevant to its performance in the system of which it is a part. A part that works well when considered separately may not work well when interacting with other parts of a system; the parts may not fit together well. A Rolls-Royce engine may not fit into a Volkswagen. A manufacturing unit that produces products without defects that are not in demand is not nearly as good as one that produces products with defects that are in demand. For these reasons, effective corporate management must focus on the *interactions* of its parts rather than on their actions taken separately. However, current organizational designs and modes of management focus on the actions of corporate parts rather than their interactions. It is assumed that if each part works well when considered separately, the corporation as a whole will, but this is not true. Supervision and command are the management of actions; coordination and integration are the management of interactions, and this requires leadership. The exercise of leadership does not necessarily require authority. (Chapter 4 is devoted to a way to organize for and facilitate effective management of interactions.)

The defining function of a system cannot be carried out by any part of the system taken separately. For example, no part of an automobile taken alone can transport people, not even its motor. Therefore, when an automobile or any system is taken apart, it loses its defining function, its essential properties. A disassembled automobile cannot transport people, and a disassembled person does not live, read, write, or do arithmetic. A disassembled brewery cannot produce, distribute, and market beer.

Furthermore, *when an essential part of a system is separated from the system of which it is a part, that part loses its ability to carry out its defining function*. For example, when the motor of an automobile is removed from that automobile, it cannot move anything, not even itself. A steering wheel removed from a car steers nothing. A hand removed from a body cannot write. A marketing department that has no manufacturing unit or units supplying it with products to sell cannot carry out its function. On the other hand, a manufacturing department whose products are not marketed by a marketing unit cannot continue to produce products for long.

The managerial implications of all this are very great. As noted above, it implies that when the performance of each part of a system taken separately is improved, the performance of the system taken as a whole may not be improved. This assertion can be proven rigorously, but we need not resort to such a proof; a simple "thought experiment" will do the trick. A "thought experiment" is one so simple that it can be conducted in one's head with transparent results.

Let's buy one each of the approximately 555 different models of automobiles available in the United States. Then we hire the best available automotive engineers and give them the following problem. Which of the cars has the best engine? Suppose they find that the Rolls-Royce does. We note this and then ask them to do the same for the transmission. They come back saying that the best is in the Mercedes. We note this also and continue until we know which car has the best of each part required for an automobile. When the list is complete we give it to the engineers and ask them to remove the parts listed from the cars listed and assemble them into "the best possible automobile." After all, it will consist of all the best parts available. The fact is that we will not even get an automobile, let alone the best one, because *the parts do not fit together. The performance of a system is not the sum of the performance of its parts taken separately, but the product of their interactions.*

In the following observation, Gary Hamel and C. K. Prahalad (1993) reflect this aspect of systems thinking as it applies to corporations:

It is possible that GM or Ford could outspend Honda in developing engine-related technologies like combustion engineering, electronic controls, and lean burn—and perhaps even attain scientific leadership in each area—but still lag [behind] Honda in terms of all-around engine performance because the U.S. companies were able to blend [coordinate and integrate the interactions of] fewer technologies. Blending requires technology generalists, systems thinking, and the capacity to optimize complex technological trade-offs. Leadership in a range of technologies may count for little and the resources expended in such a quest may remain underleveraged if a company is not good at the subtle art of blending as it is at brute-force pioneering.

Successfully integrating diverse functional skills like R&D, production, marketing, and sales is a second form of blending. Where narrow specialization and organizational chimneys exist, functional excellence is rarely translated into product excellence. . . . Again, what is required is a class of generalists who understand the interplay of skills, technologies, and functions. [p. 81]

Nevertheless, the way most enterprises are organized and managed, and the way managers are educated, fly in the face of this property of systems. For example, in most corporate planning each organizational unit initially plans for itself independently of any others. These plans are subsequently adjusted to each other and aggregated. However, the adjustments are usually directed at removing conflict between or among the parts, not at maximizing their cooperation and collective performance.

Synergy is an increase in the value of the parts of a system that derives from their being parts of the system—that is, from their interactions with other parts of the system. Such an increase in value can occur only if the parts can do something together that they cannot do alone. Put another way, synergy requires an increase in the variety of behavior available to the parts of a system. Mechanistic and organismic concepts of an enterprise are variety-reducing; a social systemic concept alone is necessarily variety-increasing.

Part 2 makes operational the abstract notions presented here by describing organizational designs that facilitate effective management of interactions and provide ways to increase the variety of behavior that parts of an enterprise can exhibit. In the Epilogue I consider how to *educate* managers so they focus on managing interactions and increasing variety.

Whole-Part Interactions: Increasing and Decreasing Variety

A system taken as a whole can affect its parts in two ways: by increasing or by decreasing the variety of the behavior they can display. For example, when a small company is acquired by a large one, the variety of things the small company can do is either increased or decreased. If this variety is not affected, then acquisition of the small company does not result in its being integrated into a larger system, but it is simply made part of a large, unsystemic aggregation, such as a holding company.

Since social systems contain purposeful systems as their principal parts, and purposeful behavior consists of choices of ends and means, social systems must either increase or decrease the variety of ends or means available to their parts. They may increase the variety of some types of behavior and reduce others. Laws, for example, may simultaneously enable people to acquire property but not to take it by force from another.

The only justification for inclusion in a system of a nonessential organization whose product or services can be obtained from an external source is that the value of that organization is increased by its acquisition. Put another way, the inclusion of a nonessential part in a system is justified only if the value of that part is greater within the system than outside it. This is a very contemporary idea. In the past the justification for including a part in a system—for example, acquiring a company—was taken to lie exclusively in what the acquired system contributed to the value of the acquiring system, not conversely. An organization each of whose parts contributes to its value may nevertheless have little value. Unless the organization contributes to the value of its parts, they will not add as much to its value as they would otherwise. For example, the value of a company that cannot employ as many workers as it needs may be minimal; its value would be increased even with disgruntled workers. However, this increase in value is small compared to what could be obtained with employees who like their work and working conditions. Parts of a system that do not gain value through their interactions with other parts of that system ought not to be part of it; they would be more valuable if outside the organization.

A major metals producer decided to diversify in the 1980s. It acquired a small high-tech company that had an exceptionally high return of investment. In its first year as part of the large corporation the acquired company's return on investment dropped precipitously. An inquiry was launched. No difference in the acquired company's performance was found other than a large payment to corporate headquarters for corporate overhead that was allocated to it. In time it became apparent to the parent company that the acquired company was gaining nothing from its owners to compensate for this increased cost. It was sold.

Also in the 1980s, the Clark Equipment Company found that its credit division would be more valuable outside the company than within it. This followed from the fact that the division would be able to acquire capital less expensively if it were located outside the company than inside. Because Clark was having financial problems at the time, its credit rating was low, hence its cost of capital high. The credit division was turned loose. Clark was then able to obtain the new credit company's services at a lower cost than it had been able to obtain them for when it was part of the company.

If social systems, including enterprises, had no effect on the value of their parts—hence the variety of choices available to them—study of these systems as a whole would have no value; we would only need to study their parts taken separately. A whole consisting of parts none of which enjoys increased value for being part of that whole is not a system, it is an aggregation of parts. The value of a system and its parts may be increased through interactions of the whole and its parts, between or among the parts, and between or among the whole and other systems with which it forms larger systems. All three types of interaction must be managed effectively if an organization is to perform well.

Whole-part interactions in mechanistically conceived organizations. In the management of systems, including enterprises, that are conceptualized mechanistically, the interests and purposes of the parts are considered to be irrelevant. The only aspect of the behavior of the parts considered to be relevant is its contribution to the value of the whole. Managers in systems so conceived consider themselves better able to judge what is of value to the whole than their subordinate organizational units and individuals are. Therefore, they practice top-down (autocratic) management. The amount of choice permitted as one descends in an organization from the top to the bottom decreases along the way until the bottom is reached, where virtually no discretion is permitted. In such an organization, behavior at all but the top level is *reactive*, determined entirely by changes in internal or environmental conditions. No choice is involved. This ideal comes close to being realized in many bureaucracies.

In an autocratic system one person or relatively small group—for example, the CEO or the executive office—has the power to make all decisions that affect the parts of the system. This constitutes a dictatorship. Most people are aware of societies that are governed dictatorially but not of the fact that within even the least autocratic societies, such organizations as prisons, armies, churches, and *corporations* are frequently ruled by dictators.

Autocratic political structures do not preclude decentralization of decision-making, but when decentralized, lower-level decisions are always subject to an override by a higher-level authority, and ultimately by the highest authority. This means that lower-level decision-makers are expected to make the same decisions that higher-level managers would make if they were making them. As a result, lower-level managers are not concerned with determining what decision is best, but what is most acceptable.

Because lower levels of management try to make decisions that they think higher levels would make were they making them, their decision-making tends to lack any creativity. Creativity involves producing decisions that are *not* expected. Therefore, autocratic organizations tend to be uncreative. What creativity they display usually derives from the executives at the top, who alone are not concerned with higher levels of authority. This is why organizations established by creative but autocratic entrepreneurs so frequently go into decline once the role of their creators diminishes.

Autocratic (mechanistically conceptualized) enterprises can be efficient in circumstances where the conditions to which they must react are limited in number, relatively simple, and predictable. However, such organizations are not able to cope effectively with unexpected and complex changes imposed on them. They cannot adapt rapidly and effectively, if at all, to such a turbulent environment as now prevails, one characterized, it will be recalled, by an increasing rate of change and complexity. Moreover, the more complex a system becomes, the more difficult it becomes for one authority to be able to keep in mind and take into account all the relevant interactions between or among its parts.

Whole-part interactions in organismically conceived organizations. Enterprises conceptualized as an organism regard some interests of their parts—usually limited to their health, safety, and welfare—as legitimate concerns of the whole. They generally provide their parts with a greater variety of choices than one conceptualized as a mechanical system, but such variety does not include choice of both ends and means, only one or the other. Furthermore, the behavior of the parts may be *responsive* as well as reactive. Responsive behavior is behavior for which another internal or external event is only necessary, not sufficient. Therefore, responsive behavior involves choice; it is codetermined by the system and the stimulating event. A person's turning on a light when it gets dark is a response to darkness, but the light's going on when the switch is turned on is a reaction. The person who turned on a light could have raised a window shade instead. The darkness was necessary but not sufficient for either choice.

Organismically conceptualized systems are autocratic either with respect to ends or means, and democratic with respect to the other. In some such organizations the parts cannot vary the outcome they pursue, the function they perform. However, they can pursue the objectives assigned to them in a variety of ways; they are free to select the means by which they will pursue them. "Management by objectives" (MBO) operates this way. Although the parts of an organization and their managers may be involved in discussion of ends to be assigned to them, the ends to be pursued are selected by a higher authority. However, the lower-level units are free to pursue them much as they see fit. Semiautonomous work groups, which are becoming commonplace in American industry, are organized in this way. [Downsizing, as it is commonly imposed on the parts of a corporation, reflects this type of political structure.

The size of a reduction in force required of an organizational unit is imposed on it from above, but the unit is frequently free to decide who is to be released. Units of a guerrilla army and political parties are often free to select the means by which they pursue ends that have been assigned to them. In effect, in such organismically conceived organizations strategic decisions are centralized and tactical decisions decentralized.

In contrast, an organismically conceived organization may permit its parts to select their objectives, but it specifies how they are to be pursued, the means to be employed. Welfare institutions—for example, hospitals, nursing homes, and schools—are usually organized in this way. The rationale behind such a distribution of power lies in the assumption that the parts (including individuals) do not know how to pursue their own objectives as well as some experts do. In health-care systems, for example, standard procedures for treating ailments or disabilities are often specified by a higher-level authority, but diagnoses and selection of the outcome to be pursued lie with a lower treating unit. In corporations, personnel or human-resource experts often consider themselves better equipped to serve the health, safety, and welfare interests of their workers than the workers themselves are. These experts determine what benefits will be offered to the workers and in some cases even determine what kind of food will be served in the company's dining room.

In these systems, tactical decision-making is centralized but strategic decision-making is decentralized.

Clearly, either type of organismically conceptualized system is better able to adapt to changes in its environment than are mechanically conceptualized systems. The system's parts can change either their means or ends in response to changes in their environment or in the system itself. Because the parts can display some choice, they are better able to deal with unpredictable change and increasing complexity. In Stafford Beer's *The Brain of the Firm* (1972), he describes how an organismically conceptualized organization can do these things. Not surprisingly, he argues that the procedures he prescribes are essential for long-term viability, survival of organizations.

What organismically conceptualized organizations cannot do is engage in *active* adaptation. Let me explain. When most of us speak of adaptation we mean *passive* response to an environmental or internal change that reduces a system's effectiveness. The passive adaptive response restores the original effectiveness or increases it. Thus, when an enterprise responds to the introduction of a new product by a competitor by bringing out a similar product, it adapts passively. Or if it responds to a competitive reduction of prices with its own price reductions, it adapts passively. In contrast, to adapt actively is to produce a change that is not a response to a decrease in effectiveness, but to a perceived opportunity to improve. It is adaptive behavior that is self-initiated, not externally stimulated. Therefore, when Federal Express initiated an overnight mail service, it adapted actively; but when its competitors, such as UPS and the U.S. Postal Service, followed suit, they adapted passively. Passive adaptation is seldom creative or innovative; active adaptation often is.

Whole-part interactions in social-systemically conceived organizations. An enterprise conceptualized as a social system should serve the purposes of both its parts and the system of which it is a part. It should enable its parts and its containing systems to do things they could not otherwise do. They enable their parts to participate directly or indirectly in the selection of both ends and means that are relevant to them. This means that enterprises conceptualized as social systems increase the variety of both the means and ends available to their parts, and this, in turn, increases the variety of behavior available to them. All this is the essence of democracy.

In such an enterprise, the organization as a whole is seen as having an obligation to its stakeholders as well as they having an obligation to it. Therefore, a democratic political structure of a system is the only one that is compatible with viewing it as a social system. In the next chapter I will argue that it is a social system's obligation to encourage and facilitate the development of its stakeholders, and this can be realized only in a completely democratic system.

The parts of a completely democratic system must be capable of more than reactive or responsive behavior; they must be able to act. Active behavior is behavior for which no other event is either necessary or sufficient. Acts, therefore, are completely self-determined, the result of choice. Choice is essential for purposeful behavior. Therefore, if the parts of a system are to be treated as purposeful, they must be given the freedom to choose, to act.

Since enterprises do contain parts that have purposes of their own, whether they are so viewed or not, to conceptualize the enterprise as anything less than a social system restricts the variety of the behavior from which its parts can choose. This results in a failure to use all the relevant capabilities of their parts.

Enterprises conceptualized and managed as social systems, and their parts, can respond to the unpredictable changes inherent in turbulent environments and can deal effectively with increasing complexity. They can expand the variety of their behavior to match or exceed the variety of the behavior of their environments because of the freedom of choice that pervades them. They are capable not only of rapid and effective passive adaptation to change but also of active adaptation. They can innovate by perceiving and exploiting opportunities for change that are internally, not externally, stimulated.

Conclusion

The way enterprises are conceptualized has a very large effect on what they do, and what they do affects the way they are conceptualized. Enterprises have always consisted of people who have purposes of their own, and they have always been part of larger systems that have purposes of their own. Nevertheless, they have not always been thought of this way, and the way they were thought of affected their behavior. Initially, they were viewed as machines because the world was thought of as a machine. This did not mean that those who managed enterprises were unaware of the fact that they employed people who had purposes of their own, but it did mean that they considered these purposes to be irrelevant to the way they managed and the way their enterprises behaved. They looked on and treated their employees as replaceable machines or machine parts. Work was so designed that those engaged to do it behaved as though they were machines or machine parts. This is what made Taylor's so-called scientific management (1911) possible. Time-and-motion studies were based on the assumption that people could be effectively thought of and managed as though they were machines.

The parts of enterprises conceptualized as organisms, and the enterprises themselves, can adapt to turbulence and increasing complexity better than mechanistically conceptualized systems and their parts. They have more flexibility because they can respond differently to the same stimulus; machines can't. But the parts of enterprises conceptualized as social systems, and the enterprises themselves, are best able to deal with turbulence. Not only can they respond to it more effectively than the other types of systems but also they can convert what to others constitute threats to their survival, into opportunities for "thrival," continuous development. The next chapter focuses on the nature of development and how to encourage and facilitate it.

In this chapter I focused more on the implications of the systemic aspects of an enterprise than on its social aspects. (This imbalance is also corrected in the next chapter.) To be sure, machines and organisms are also systems. However, the systemic character of enterprises viewed as machines or organisms is not thought about as deeply as when they are viewed as social systems. Most managers are still unaware of the implications of the systemic properties of enterprises. Perhaps most important among these implications is the fact that the performance of a system is not the sum of the performances of its parts taken separately; it is the product of their interactions. Therefore, the focus of management should be on the way the parts of an enterprise interact, not act taken separately, and on how the enterprise interacts with other systems in its environment. Enterprises are not currently organized to facilitate managers focusing on interactions, only on the actions of parts taken separately. Furthermore, their compensation normally provides incentives only for improving the actions of parts, not their interactions. How to organize to manage interactions effectively is the subject of Chapter 4.

Improving the performance of the parts of a system taken separately may not, and often does not, improve the performance of the system taken as a whole. This implies that in designing a system the properties of the parts should be derived from the properties designed into the whole. Too frequently, the properties designed into an enterprise as a whole are derived from the properties of their parts. How to design enterprises properly is discussed in Chapter 3.

The only justification for including a part in a system is either that it contributes to the value of the whole or that its value is enhanced by such inclusion. If a nonessential part of a system has less value as part of that system than it would have outside it, it should be released. If it can have no more value outside than inside, but the system can obtain its output less expensively from external suppliers, it should be allowed to migrate or disappear. How such determinations should be made is the subject of Chapter 5.

It will become increasingly apparent as this book continues that I believe that corporations conceptualized as machines or organisms cannot thrive in the emerging turbulent global economy. They must be viewed, organized, and managed as social systems if they are to survive, let alone thrive.

The social-systemic view of an enterprise is based on considering three "levels" of purpose: the purposes of the larger system of which an enterprise is a part, the purposes of the enterprise itself, and the purposes of its parts. In the next chapter I consider each of these purposes in turn, and how they can be served effectively.

Chapter 2

The Enterprise and Its Stakeholders

Since an enterprise conceptualized as a social system involves three major sets of purposes—those of its containing system, its own, and those of its parts—it can be viewed from each of these perspectives. These views are different but compatible. First, I consider the role of the corporation in the larger system of which it is a part, society. What societal purposes do corporations have the function of furthering? Then I consider the nature of the overriding purpose of corporations conceptualized as social systems, development, and what is required of an organization for continuous development.

The meaning of "development" is discussed in detail later in this chapter. At this point, however, it is important to keep in mind that development and growth are not the same thing; they are not even necessary for each other. Either can take place without the other. Growth is an increase in size or number. Development is an increase in capability, competence.

The Role of the Corporation in Society

All corporations operate within at least one society. They are also parts of such other systems as industry associations and chambers of commerce. Of all the systems of which corporations are a part, societies have the greatest effect on them because in general they can exercise more control over the corporations operating within them than can any of the other containing systems.

The societal view of enterprises as social systems focuses on those they affect *directly*, their stakeholders, and the ways they are affected. This concern is reflected in what has come to be known as the "stakeholder theory of the firm." According to Igor Ansoff (1965):

> This theory maintains that the objectives of the firm should be derived from balancing the conflicting claims of the various "stakeholders" in the firm: managers, workers, stockholders, suppliers, vendors. The firm has a responsibility to all of these and must configure its objectives so as to give each a measure of satisfaction. Profit which is a return on investment to the stockholder is one of such satisfactions, but does not receive special predominance in the objective structure. [p. 34]

A version of this theory, perhaps the first, was formulated by Cyert and March (1963).

The stakeholders may include more parties than Ansoff identified—for example, customers, consumers, creditors, debtors, and government. Competitors are not included because they are not affected *directly* by what an enterprise does. They are affected indirectly by the effects of an enterprise on others, such as, suppliers, customers, and distributors. Unless these others are affected, competitors cannot be.

Different enterprises may have different kinds of stakeholders. For example, some producers of goods have wholesalers, retailers, and independent sales agents as stakeholders.

Others do their own distributing and selling. Those who out-source some or all of their production have their suppliers as stakeholders. Fortunately, the essential characteristics of the stakeholder view of a firm do not depend on the kinds of stakeholder involved, only on their existence, whatever their roles. This will become apparent as this view of the firm is developed. To do so, I use a simple enterprise, one with only six types of stakeholders. However, as will become apparent, a much larger number may be involved.

The types of stakeholder I consider are:

1. *employees* and others (such as consultants) who do work for the enterprise;
2. *suppliers* of goods and services;
3. *customers,* who, in this example, I assume are the ultimate *consumers* as well (they need not be the same: Retailers may be the customers of a product-producing company; the retailers' customers may be the consumers);
4. *investors and creditors;*
5. *debtors;*
6. *government and the public.*

The Stakeholder View of the Firm

This view of the firm can be grasped by imagining a visitor to Earth who is sent down from another planet to find out what a business enterprise is here. The visitor has no knowledge of any language used on Earth and therefore can't converse with anyone, nor read any of the relevant literature. All the visitor can do is observe what enterprises do. What is observed approximates the stakeholder view of the firm (Fig. 2.1).

First, there is a group of people who put their labor into the firm and take money out. This group obviously includes those we call *employees,* but it also includes consultants, external auditors, invited speakers, and so on. Second, the visitor

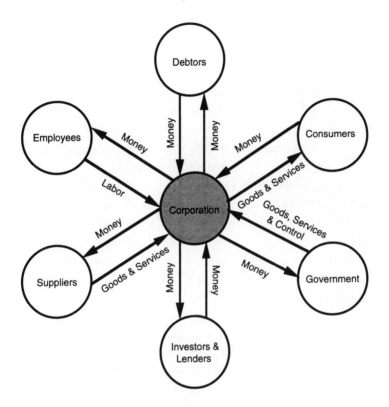

Fig. 2.1. A stakeholder view of the firm.

also sees organizations and individuals who provide the firm with goods and services, and who receive money in return. These are the *suppliers*. Third, *customers* are the converse of suppliers; they are supplied with goods and services by the firm in exchange for money. In most cases the goods and services provided by the firm to customers are not the same as those provided to it by its suppliers; firms generally process what they receive to add value to it. In the case of a retail store or other firm whose activity is solely distribution and marketing, the value it adds to the products it receives lies in increasing their accessibility to customers.

Fourth, *investors* (for example, stockholders) and creditors (for example, banks that lend money to the firm) put money into the firm and subsequently receive money in return, but the amount taken out usually differs from the amount put in, and the insertions and withdrawals are spread over time. Fifth, *debtors* are the opposite. They use the firm's resources for a fee. These include banks in which the firm deposits its operating capital, companies whose stock the firm owns, and so on. Finally, there is the *government*, representing the affected public. It, too, provides goods (such as water and roads) and services (such as police and fire protection) in exchange for money (usually paid in the form of taxes but sometimes as fees, as for licenses). Although it is not necessary to do so, I treat government as distinct from suppliers for two reasons. First, it has some control over the behavior of the firm; other suppliers do not. Second, the goods and services that government provides do not normally become the property of the firm even though it uses them.

In this particular stakeholder view of a very simple firm there are six types of stakeholder and therefore twelve flows, six in and six out. Examination of these flows reveals that they are of two types: Enterprises consume resources (for example, labor, money, and goods), and they make consumption possible—directly, by providing products and services, and indirectly, by providing money with which goods and services can be purchased. If we subtract the value of what a firm consumes from the value of the consumption it makes possible, the difference is the *wealth* it creates. Therefore, from society's point of view, an obvious function of corporations is to *produce wealth*. What is not so obvious is that corporations also have the social function of *distributing wealth*. They do so in a number of ways, including compensating employees for work, paying suppliers for the goods and services they provide, providing dividends to shareholders, paying taxes and interest on money borrowed, and so on.

The compensation provided by an enterprise to those whose work adds value to what they work on is the only known way to produce and distribute wealth simultaneously. All other ways of distributing wealth (for example, welfare, pensions, and subsidies) involve net consumption of it. This endows productive employment with a unique role in society. Unemployment is a (if not *the*) principal producer of political unrest. It frequently leads to a change of government, peacefully or otherwise. Governments know this. Therefore, when employment in the private sector begins to decrease significantly, governments have frequently intervened to create or maintain employment by nationalizing those companies that have gone, or are about to go, out of business. The principal objective of nationalization of a company or an industry is not to maximize its profit but to maintain if not maximize its employment.

In 1976, while I was on a sabbatical year in Mexico, I conducted a study to determine why Pemex, the nationalized oil monopoly in that country, was losing money despite what seemed to be conditions made for profitability. I found the answer: The company employed several people for every job it had. When I pointed this out to a deputy minister of National Patrimony, the branch of government responsible for nationalized industries, he said, "Of course. That is the purpose of the company. The government is not threatened by a lack of profit from Pemex, but it would be if Pemex were to cut employment back to only the number it needed to operate efficiently."

Governments can survive a great deal more deficit spending, corruption, and inefficiency than unemployment. In addition, by taking over private enterprises, governments can also "make work"—that is, create jobs that have little or no useful output—for example, operators of automatic elevators and starters in elevator lobbies who push the up and down buttons for those waiting. Red tape is a common product of those who have no useful work to do. Unfortunately, red tape and other products of make-work obstruct those who have useful work to do.

Work that has no useful output permeates bureaucracies. They are generally inefficient and can seldom survive competition. Therefore they are frequently found in monopolies created or protected by government—for example, public utilities and service organizations. However, bureaucracies are also common in monopolies created within corporations—for example, in such internal service units as accounting, finance, legal, and R&D. (I will focus on such monopolies and how to eliminate them in Chapter 5.)

Communist states are saturated with bureaucratic monopolies, systems that produce make-work rather than make work productive. This is a major reason that they have not been able to produce enough wealth to satisfy those they govern. However, capitalist societies are not immune to the bureaucratic threat: The increase of bureaucratic monopolies within private enterprises threatens their productivity and therefore their ability to compete in global markets.

Ironically, in the past, the failure of private enterprises to provide enough employment to distribute wealth equitably has been the principal producer of communism and socialism. Recently, the converse has been the case: The failure of communism to produce enough wealth to be distributed has been the principal producer of reversions to capitalism. The point of all this is that *the creation of productive employment* is an extremely important societal function of private enterprises seen as social systems.

Downsizing might possibly be excusable if it were successful. But a 1992 survey of 1,204 companies conducted by Right Associates showed that this is not the case (Knox, 1992): "Corporate downsizing has a lot in common with dieting: Nearly everyone does it, but few get the desired results. Three out of four companies slimmed down their staffs in the last five years, but the majority saw little improvement in either business or productivity . . ." (p. Dl).

These observations were echoed by Peter Drucker (1991): "Scores of large organizations—businesses of all kinds but also government agencies, hospitals and universities—have sharply cut staffs these past few years. But few have realized the expected cost savings. In some cases costs have even gone up. In many more performance has suffered . . ." (p. Al0).

Creative alternatives to downsizing and rightsizing are available. For example, one company that was on the verge of bankruptcy found it could purchase transportation of its products to its distributors from outside trucking companies at a lower cost than its then-current trucking unit could provide it for. The main reason for the difference in cost was that because of pay scales established by the company's union, the company payed its drivers more than external trucking firms payed theirs. Rather than fire the drivers and the others in the internal transportation department, the company's CEO called them into a meeting and told them why it was necessary for the company to outsource its transportation. Then he showed them how much it would cost the company to discharge those present. He then suggested that the money involved be pooled and that a bank loan be obtained that would enable the employees to buy out the department. They could then establish a new trucking company, which he would give an extended contract for transporting the company's products on the condition that its charges for doing so would be no greater than those of other commercial carriers. This suggestion was accepted, the necessary financing was obtained with the company's help, and the new trucking company was established and has since done very well. No one lost employment.

Several years ago the CEO of a major corporation in the United States became interested in the stakeholder view of the firm and asked the university-based research group of which I was then a part if the importance of his corporation, from society's point of view, to each of its stakeholder groups—not their importance to the corporation—could be estimated. A study was designed to do this. Starting with the employees, it was argued that, all other things being equal, the more people employed by an enterprise, the greater its value to society, and the higher the average percentage of their incomes that employees derive from compensation for work performed for the enterprise, the greater its value to society as well as to its employees. Therefore, the product of these two numbers was used as an index of the importance of the enterprise to its employees from society's and their point of view.

Similarly, the importance of the company to its customers was represented by the number of customers it had times the average percentage of their disposable income spent on the company's products and services. Similar indices were developed for each stakeholder group.

The result of this analysis was surprising. From society's point of view the importance of the firm to its employees was greater than its combined importance to the next four stakeholder groups. Therefore, it was argued that from society's point of view the enterprise involved in this study has a much greater obligation to its employees than to any other stakeholder group. Whether this is true in general remains to be determined.

It follows from all this that a principal social obligation of an enterprise—whether publicly or privately owned—is to maintain, if not create, employment. However, in the current highly competitive global marketplace, it is apparent that the only enterprises that can survive in the long run are those that can continually increase their productivity. But to increase productivity one must usually decrease the labor required per unit of output. Therefore, the requirements for greater productivity and for stable or increasing employment appear to be in conflict. Fortunately, this is not the case; with growth both can occur simultaneously Therefore, in an enterprise seen as a social system, growth is taken to be a means, not an end. The end, as previously noted, is *development*.

Development vs. Growth

Despite the fact that "growth" and "development" are often treated as synonyms, as previously noted, they are not the same thing. Neither is required for the other. A rubbish heap grows but does not develop, and a person can develop without growing.

Growth is an increase in size or number. *Development is an ability and desire to satisfy one's own needs and legitimate desires and those of others*. A legitimate desire is one the satisfaction of which does not inhibit the development of someone else. Therefore, a desire to incapacitate another or to deprive him or her of a needed resource is not legitimate. A *need* is a requirement for well-being or survival; for example, food and oxygen are needed by organisms. A *desire* is a "conscious impulse toward something that promises enjoyment or satisfaction in its attainment" (*Merriam-Webster's Collegiate Dictionary*, 10th ed. [1993], p. 313). We may or may not desire what we need, and needs, unlike desires, may be unconscious. For example, people may not desire calcium in their diets because they are unconscious of their need for it. On the other hand, people may have even very strong desires for things that they do not need, even things that harm them, such as addictive drugs.

Purposeless things—for example, inanimate objects, plants, and lower-level animals—can grow but not develop; only purposeful entities can develop because they alone have desires and the ability to satisfy them.

Development is an increase in an entity's potential, not necessarily in its actual attainments. It has less to do with how much one has than with how much one can do with whatever one has. It is more a matter of learning than earning. Robinson

Crusoe and the Swiss family Robinson are better models of development than John D. Rockefeller and J. Pierpont Morgan.

Because development involves increases of desire and ability, one person or organization cannot give or impose it on another. Contrary to popular belief, a government cannot develop the governed, and a corporation cannot develop its employees. Because development is a learning process, one person cannot learn for another. To be taught and to learn are very different things. Md. Anisur Rahman (1991) described the evolution of his thinking from the belief that development can be *given* to a people to the belief that it can only be *taken* by them:

> Knowledge cannot be transferred—it can only be memorized for mechanical application, but learning is always an act of self-search and discovery. In this search and discovery one may be stimulated and assisted but cannot be "taught." Nor can one be "trained" to perform tasks which are not mechanical but creative. Institutions of teaching and training which seek to transfer knowledge and skills serve mostly to disorient the capacity that is in every healthy individual to creatively search and discover knowledge. [p. 25]

The only kind of development that is possible is *self-*development. Nevertheless, one person or organization can encourage and facilitate the development of others. For example, although teachers cannot learn subjects for their students, they can encourage and facilitate their learning.

The economic growth of a society is best reflected in its *standard of living;* its development is best reflected in its *quality of life*. Wealth is a measure of standard of living, not quality of life. An increase in wealth can actually decrease one's quality of life. If we were to ship electric appliances and automobiles to aborigines, we would not increase their development. On the other hand, if we were to educate them, they would develop even if we did not give them any additional resources. The more developed persons or organizations are, the more they can do with whatever resources they have, and the more resources they can create or find.

It has become increasingly apparent that when standards of living increase, quality of life may decrease. On the other hand, quality of life can increase without an increase in standard of living—in fact, even when it decreases. This is not to say that wealth is irrelevant to development or quality of life; it is very relevant. How much people can improve their quality of life and that of others depends not only on their desire and ability to do so, but also on the resources available to them—that is, it depends on both their level of development and their standard of living. The quality of life that people can actually attain is the product of both their development and the quality and quantity of resources available to them, their wealth. A better house can be built with good tools and materials than with poor ones. However, a well-developed person with limited resources can often build a better house than a poorly developed person with more resources.

When corporations assume the role in society of producing and distributing wealth, they contribute to the development of society and its members. It does not develop them, but it does facilitate and encourage their development.

As Meadows et al. (1972) argued, a lack of resources can limit growth and increases in the standard of living, but it cannot limit development and improvement of the quality of life. The more developed an entity is, the less it is limited by available resources. Nevertheless, the more resources a society and its members have, the more rapidly they can develop.

The Developmental Ideal

Competence is the ability to satisfy needs and desires; therefore it is the output, the product, of development. An unlimited ability to satisfy one's needs and desires and those of others can be called *omnicompetence*. Unlike *omnipotence*, which connotes power *over* others, their control; omnicompetence connotes power *to* satisfy oneself and others, self-control. Omnipotence connotes an ability to constrain or restrict others; omnicompetence connotes an ability to empower others.

The American philosopher E. A. Singer, Jr. (1923 and 1948), pointed out that the unlimited ability to satisfy needs and desires is an ideal of all people—past, present, and future. No matter what people desire, they must want the ability to obtain it. This is true even for those who want to eliminate all desire and attain Nirvana. Those who seek Nirvana have needs that must be satisfied if they are to attain and experience it. The only way to avoid needs is to commit suicide, but one cannot even desire to end one's life without wanting the ability to do so.

Omnicompetence is an *ideal* because, although it can never be attained, it can be approached continually. Therefore, progress toward this ideal is not limited. Because the attainment of omnicompetence implies the ability to attain all one's ends, including all other ideals, it is a *meta*-ideal, the ultimate ideal. Omnicompetence is an adult word for the wish children often express when they hear the story granting three wishes; they wish that all their wishes would come true. They don't need the other two wishes.

From the social systemic point of view, corporations have an obligation to encourage and facilitate the development of society and their stakeholders. An enterprise develops to the extent that it increases its ability and desire to encourage and facilitate the development of others, society, and the enterprise's stakeholders. Note that when an organization or an individual adopts the development of others as its principal objective, altruism and egotism are completely merged.

To understand how an enterprise can contribute to the development of others it is necessary to understand generally what is required to sustain it, its "dimensions."

The "Dimensions" of Development

Ancient Greek philosophers identified four pursuits each of which is separately necessary but that, only when taken together are sufficient for continuous development. These are the pursuits of *truth, plenty, the good,* and *beauty/fun*.

Truth. The pursuit of truth is the societal function of scientific and technological institutions. Science discovers truth, and technology puts it to use. Together they develop and make available such information, knowledge, and understanding as enable people to pursue their ends more *efficiently*. The information, knowledge, and understanding produced by science and technology are disseminated by educational institutions.

Plenty. The pursuit of plenty is a function of a variety of institutions that are concerned with (1) producing and distributing the resources that enable us to pursue our ends as efficiently as we know how (economic institutions), and (2) protecting resources acquired against their appropriation, theft, or destruction by others or nature (e.g., the justice system, the health system, flood control, the military, and insurance).

The Good. The pursuit of the good is the function of institutions that disseminate ethical and moral principles—for example, religious and educational institutions, and more recently, psychiatry. (Mental-health-care providers have entered the ethical-moral domain only in the recent past.) Ethics and morality are directed at removing *conflict* within, between, and among individuals and groups; their objectives are *peace of mind* and *peace on Earth*. People in conflict have conflicting objectives. Conflicting objectives are ones that cannot be attained simultaneously. Therefore, the reduction of such conflict is necessary for continuous progress toward omnicompetence, an ability to satisfy *all* our needs and desires.

Beauty/Fun. The pursuits of beauty and fun are inseparable aspects of aesthetics. They make possible the continuous pursuit of ideals that, you will recall, are ends that can never be attained. They induce people to pursue such ends despite their unattainability.

The role of aesthetics is not as well understood in our culture as are the roles of science, technology, education, and economics, or even as well as ethics-morality. The importance of ethics and morality is slowly coming to be appreciated. Most business schools now have courses on the subject, however vacuous they may be. "Management science," "management technology," "management education," and "management ethics" are expressions that have some meaning for most of us. On the other hand, the "aesthetics of management" conveys no meaning to most of us.

The emergence of aesthetics as a very important dimension of development and a very important aspect of management is a recent phenomenon, one that is closely associated with systems thinking, understanding the meaning of development systemically.

From Efficiency to Effectiveness: Adding Value

Science, technology, and economics focus on *efficiency*, not *effectiveness*. The efficiency of a course of action relative to a possible outcome in a specified environment is measured in one of two ways: either the probability that it will produce that outcome in that environment, or the amount of resources it consumes in producing that outcome in that environment. For example, given two production processes that produce the same type of product, the one that is more likely to produce ones that meet standards is said to be more efficient. In other words, its probability of producing an acceptable product is higher. Alternatively, of two production processes that turn out equivalent products, the one that does so at the lower cost is said to be more efficient.

The effectiveness of a course of action in a specified environment is a function of its efficiency for each possible outcome and *the values of these outcomes to those affected by them.* A very efficient men's clothing manufacturer may with great efficiency turn out suits that do not fit well. Another, less efficient manufacturer may turn out suits that do fit well. Because "fit" is a value to customers, the second manufacturer would be considered to be more effective even though less efficient. Of course, a manufacturer could be both more efficient and more effective.

The value of an end is not included in the meaning of the efficiency of the means with which it is pursued, but it is included in the meaning of the effectiveness of that pursuit. *Effectiveness is evaluated efficiency*—that is, efficiency weighted by the value of its product. The efficiency of an act can be determined without reference to those affected by it. Not so for effectiveness. It is very personal. The value of an act is never independent of those affected by it, and therefore may be quite different for different individuals.

The difference between efficiency and effectiveness is reflected in the difference between growth and development. Growth does not necessarily imply an increase in value; development does. The recent deterioration of General Motors and IBM shows that companies that grow do not necessarily develop. A company can grow but cannot develop without increasing its value.

Value is the subject matter of ethics and aesthetics. Therefore, they are necessarily involved in the conversion of efficiency into effectiveness. The production of information, knowledge, and understanding is primarily a function of science. The production of wisdom, which presupposes all three, is primarily a function of ethics and aesthetics because their essential contribution to human progress is the insertion of values into conscious human decision-making. Efficiency is the product of information, knowledge, and understanding; effectiveness is the product of wisdom. Wisdom enlarges the focus of decision-making from efficiency to effectiveness. It enlarges the range of possible consequences of a decision that are taken into account, and the length of time over which it is taken to have possible consequences. By taking long- as well as short-run consequences into account, it prevents the future being sacrificed for the present.

Since wisdom adds value to consideration of efficiency, it is important to understand value as least as well as we understand efficiency. This is not yet the case, but our understanding of value, ethical-moral and aesthetic, is increasing under pressure from systemic thinking and our growing preoccupation with development.

Ethics-Morality

"Ethics" and "morality" are normally treated as synonyms. For example, *Merriam-Webster's Collegiate Dictionary*, 10th ed., (1993), defines "ethic" as "the discipline dealing with what is good and bad and with moral duty and obligation," and also as "a set of moral principles or values" (p. 398). It defines "moral" as "sanctioned by or operative on one's conscience or ethical judgment." This dictionary also gives "ethical" as a synonym for "moral." It goes on to say that "ethical" may suggest the involvement of more difficult or subtle questions of rightness, fairness, or equity" (p. 756). Despite this, I have failed to find a generally accepted difference between them. This, it seems to me, leaves me free to differentiate them (or not) as I see fit. I tend to think of ethics as dealing with principles that are transsocietal, that are intended to apply to everyone, regardless of what society they are part of; and morality as principles are generated by a society and may apply only to it.

Most ethicists believe that the function of ethics is to specify what ends should be pursued and how. This is reflected in two traditional approaches to the subject: one mechanistic and the other organismic.

Mechanistic ethics. The mechanistic approach to ethics involves the formulation of rigid rules of conduct, much like a computer program. Adherence to these rules is taken to constitute the good; virtue equals conformity. The Ten Commandments, the Golden Rule, and Kant's Categorical Imperative are examples of such rules.

When the good consists of conformity to rules, violation of a rule is taken to be bad. There are no "in betweens." This invariably gives rise to ethical dilemmas, problems of choice that cannot be resolved given a particular set of rules. This is even true of the Ten Commandments. For example, honoring a parent who commits adultery, or not killing someone who is about to kill a parent, creates an ethical dilemma for adherents to the Commandments.

However, there are other more serious difficulties with equating the good to conformity to rules. Who authenticates the rules? The usual answer has been "God." What assurance do we have that those who claim to speak in his name are authorized to do so by him? How do we account for the incompatibility of ethical rules derived from different concepts of God? Which God is authenticated, how, and by whom?

There are substantial inconsistencies among the ethics of different religions. Bertrand Russell (in Egner, 1958) pointed this out with vigor:

> Protestants tell us, or used to tell us, that it is contrary to the will of God to work on Sundays. But Jews say that it is on Saturdays that God objects to work. Disagreement on this point has per-

sisted for nineteen centuries, and I know no method of putting an end to the disagreement except Hitler's lethal chambers, which would not generally be regarded as a legitimate method in scientific controversy. Jews and Mohammedans assure us that God forbids pork, but Hindus say that it is beef that he forbids. Disagreement on this point has caused hundreds of thousands to be massacred in recent years. It can hardly be said, therefore, that the will of God gives a basis for an objective ethic. [pp. 114–15]

Who is to determine whether behavior conforms to rules? There are difficulties in many such determinations because good and bad—like conformity and nonconformity—are matters of degree, not black or white. For example, does exaggeration or understatement constitute a lie? Does failure to follow a parent's bad advice constitute a failure to honor the parent?

Conscience has also been widely accepted as an authenticator of ethical and moral laws, but it provides no better answers to questions similar to those asked about the role of God. Whose conscience authenticates? How do we deal with conflicting dictates of different consciences? And so on.

Organismic ethics. An alternative to mechanistic ethics—which considers human purposes to be irrelevant in determining what is good—is an ethics that accepts *survival* as the principal objective of purposeful entities, and therefore as the ultimate good. Then it follows that whatever contributes to survival is good. This reduces goodness to efficiency with respect to survival.

Such an ethics raises questions that are as difficult to answer as those raised by mechanistic ethics. For example, which evaluation should prevail when what is efficient for one person is inefficient for another? When an act is good for a short-run objective but bad for one that is long-run, or vice versa, which evaluation should prevail? How does one handle the desire to die of persons suffering intensely from a terminal illness, particularly when they are using resources to stay alive that could be used to keep another person alive for a much longer time? How can one justify war ethically, as most leaders of nations at war and even religious leaders do? Questions like these seem to suggest there is something more valuable than life itself.

Organismic ethics are necessarily relativistic: What is efficient/good for one person may not be efficient/good for another. This generalizes to cultural relativism: What is good in one society may not be in another. This is consistent with anthropological findings that there is not a single ethical principle that is universally adhered to—that is, in all societies. For example, in some Eskimo societies it has been the responsibility of the oldest son to place aging parents on an ice floe, where they will perish. This is required in a society where food is scarce and must be rationed to the young.

The principal problem with organismic ethics is that it provides no ethical basis for the resolution or dissolution of conflict between or among individuals or groups. What is conducive to the survival of one party may threaten the survival of another. What works for one may not work for another. Yet there does seem to be some justification for an ethics that takes into account individual, environmental, and cultural differences. Social-systemic ethics does so without raising the dilemmas associated with organismic ethics.

Social-systemic ethics. These ethics are based on recognition of the fact that social systems (1) have purposes of their own, (2) contain individuals who have purposes of their own, (3) are part of larger systems that have purposes of their own, and (4) these larger containing systems contain other social systems and individuals with purposes of their own. In addition, it is based on the concept of purpose as choice of both ends and means, and recognition of the fact that individual and group purposes may change over time and in different environments.

Every attainable end is itself a means to a more general end. We glue two pieces of wood together (means) to build a bookcase (end). We build the bookcase (means) to store books (end). We store books (means) to gain knowledge (end), and so forth. This creates a problem if we are going to evaluate ethically a choice of means by its consequences. Since every choice of means has a chain of consequences, which one do we use? It seems reasonable to answer: the ultimate consequence. Is there an ultimate consequence that we can say is good because it *must* be desired by every individual who has lived and who ever will live?

If there were such an end, then it would appear that all ethical evaluations could be made relative to it. *The meta-ideal of development, omnicompetence, is just such an end.* (Recall that one cannot want anything without wanting the ability to obtain it.) Therefore, it follows from this line of thinking that behavior that encourages and facilitates the development of others can be taken to be ethically good. However, we cannot encourage and facilitate the development of others unless we know what their needs and objectives are. Unfortunately, we can never know all the relevant needs and desires of others. Nevertheless, there is a way out of this dilemma, a way that denies an implicit assumption made by all traditional ethics.

Mechanistic (absolute) and organismic (relativistic) ethics respectively evaluate decisions by their content (conformity to rule) and their consequences, their outputs. Instead, suppose we evaluate decisions by what goes into them, not by what comes out of them. This is precisely what a social-systemic ethics does: It evaluates decisions *by the way they are made and by whom*, not by their content or consequences.

Recall that learning is the process of development. There is no better way to learn how to satisfy one's own needs and legitimate desires and those of others than by engaging with others in making decisions and evaluating their consequences. This does not preclude making mistakes, fortunately. Fortunately, because we learn from mistakes rather than from doing things right. When what we do turns out to be right, all we get is confirmation of what we already know. But when we make a mistake, determine its cause, and correct for it, we learn and develop. Therefore, when we say that it is a responsibility of an enterprise to develop its members, this implies providing them with an opportunity to participate in decisions that can affect their competence, that enable them to develop. How this can be done is the subject of Chapter 4.

Social-systemic ethics requires answering these questions: "Who should be involved in making decisions?" and "How should they be made?" Only the first of these questions is addressed in this chapter. The second question is also addressed in Chapter 4.

The who-should-be-involved question is answered by what might be called the "participative principle": *Either all those who are directly affected by a decision, the decision's stakeholders, or representatives they select, should be involved in making that decision.* Clearly, the number of stakeholders of some corporate or governmental decisions runs into millions, and there is no practical way of involving them directly in every decision that affects them directly. It is not even practical to conduct a referendum on every corporate and public issue that arises. Therefore, stakeholder representatives must be used.

If those represented are to be considered to have a voice in decision-making in which they do not participate directly, they must be able to select their representatives and recall them whenever they desire. This would extend the current practice of having stockholder representatives on corporate boards to including representatives of all other stakeholders on these boards. An increasing number of corporations are already doing so. Some corporations have created special boards consisting of representatives of such other stakeholder groups as customers, wholesalers, or retailers, and having them advise their corporate boards on issues that affect those represented.

Young people and those who are yet to be born are stakeholders in many corporate decisions, particularly ones that affect what their environment will be. Yet they are unable to speak for themselves or even select representatives. People selected to represent them cannot possibly know what they are going to want in the future; they generally don't even know what they themselves will want in the future. As a result, the young and the yet-to-be-born are almost always ignored in decision-making. Clearly, their interests should be taken into account, but since we do not know what their interests will be, what can be done about it? This, it should be noted, is a very important ethical question.

We do know one thing about the young and future generations: They, like us, will prefer to make their own decisions, rather than having them made for them. Therefore they should be allowed to decide for themselves. *This requires our keeping their options open.* If anything, we should increase their options, not decrease them. Today, however, we frequently make decisions that reduce the range of choices that will be available to those who will occupy the future.

For example, future options are significantly reduced by destruction and pollution of our physical environment, extinction of species of plants and animals, and exhaustion of limited natural resources. War—perhaps the most destructive of human activities—removes some or all future options for many. We have no right to deprive future generations of the things they might need or desire, however much we may need or desire them.

But how, one may well ask, can one use a nonrenewable natural resource such as oil without reducing options available to future generations? By conserving as much oil as we can and by developing alternative sources of energy. We clearly have an obligation to see to it that renewable resources are renewed. We can also use limited resources in a way that does not preclude their conversion to other uses in the future. For example, when we build buildings, we "use up" land that often cannot be used for other purposes without incurring prohibitive costs. However, we have the ability to construct buildings that can be disassembled and moved with relative ease. This is apparent when we examine what has happened to the structures and sites of previous world fairs.

In many of our decisions we do not even take into account our own future needs and desires. When many decision-makers consider ethical values at all, they generally restrict their considerations to the short run, and sacrifice the long run for it. Wise decision-makers effectively balance short- and long-run interests. They do so by making decisions that meet short-run requirements but that keep open as many of their future options as possible. For example, we construct buildings that are usually designed on the assumption that their use will not change over time. Therefore they are built rigidly, hence are difficult to change. Yet there is hardly a building that does not undergo significant modification within a few years after its completion. We know how to design and construct buildings that allow for almost unlimited changes at a relatively low cost and without much effort. (Consider the flexibility we build into stages of theaters and convention halls.) Of course, flexible buildings may initially cost more than rigid buildings, but when the costs of future modifications are taken into account, the higher costs incurred now are usually more than offset by savings in the future.

Renewal of resources and flexibility of the artifacts in which they are used are keys to keeping options available to future generations. Flexibility is important even in the design of products, particularly ones such as computers, which are subject to rapid technological obsolescence. Those who purchased personal computers a few years ago did not have their interests well served when, by the time their computers and they were "broken in," new models had been brought out that were significantly better than the old ones, and their old models could not be upgraded. Some computer manufacturers have made improvements that can be installed in old equipment to upgrade it. This shows a concern with future interests of current stakeholders.

Future-impact-assessment studies should be made of all decisions that have more than short-term consequences. Such studies would not differ much from currently conducted environmental-impact studies, except that they would focus on the effects on stakeholders rather than on the environment. Also, unlike environmental-impact studies, they should be monitored and followed up systematically. Once future-impact studies and the decisions based on them have been made, the predicted effects of these decisions on the stakeholders and the assumptions on which these predictions are based should be monitored closely and continually. Whenever either the assumptions or the actual effects of these decisions are observed to deviate significantly from what was expected, the decisions should be reviewed and modified as required. These activities should be incorporated into learning-support systems that are provided by enterprises. Such systems would enable the organizations as well as their members to learn and adapt more rapidly and effectively.

The freedom to decide, to make choices, may well be the most precious freedom people can have. If learning—hence development—is to be maximized, the freedom to make mistakes, learn from them, and try again must go along with the ability to choose. But all this is futile without alternatives from which to choose. To deprive future generations of options is to deprive them of choice and hence the opportunity to develop. And this is social-systemically immoral.

Social-systemic ethics clearly have important implications for corporate behavior. First, they imply providing all those who have a stake in corporate decisions with an opportunity to participate directly or indirectly in making them. Second, they require monitoring the decisions made to be sure that future options are not closed but, if anything, are increased. In addition, the decisions should be monitored to determine if they were mistaken; if so, why; and then corrections made—all this to maximize learning from decisions made. Social-systemic ethics imply the right to make mistakes and to try again. Finally, they require increasing future options or keeping them open for the young and those yet to be born—not depriving them of any of the freedom of choice we have.

August A. Busch III, CEO of Anheuser-Busch, Inc., once told the executives reporting to him: "If you didn't make a mistake last year you didn't try anything new and you didn't learn anything. I want you to try new things and, therefore, make mistakes. A mistake made once will never be held against you, but making the same mistake twice will."

Aesthetics

As I have already observed, the pursuit of beauty is the least understood of the four requirements of development, particularly among corporations. Most people, including executives and managers, would agree that at least some Western societies (including ours) have made scientific, technological, and economic progress. Perhaps fewer, but some, would argue that ethical progress has also been made. However, hardly anyone would argue that we have made aesthetic progress—that we can either produce better art or appreciate natural or man-made beauty more than our predecessors did. Moreover, there has been little agreement historically on what the nature or function of aesthetics is. And as I have also previously noted, few managers or management educators have any concept of managerial or corporate aesthetics.

In *The Republic,* Plato wrote that art was a potentially dangerous stimulant that threatens the stability of society. He saw art as a producer of dissatisfaction with the way things are and therefore as disruptive of the status quo. Therefore he took art to be a thorn in the side of his utopian republic.

For most of us, an unchanging society, even Plato's republic, could not be ideal. We prefer a dynamic state in which there are unlimited numbers of both problems yet to be solved and objectives yet to be pursued. This preference is based on the fact that we derive at least as much satisfaction from seeking solutions to problems and pursuing objectives as we do from attaining them. An ideal state is not one, again like Plato's republic, in which we already have everything we want, but one in which there is always something more to be had, and in which we have the ability and the desire to obtain it. Most of us do not conceptualize a utopia as a state in which no striving is required, but one in which all striving is fruitful. It is a state in which continuous development would be possible. Therefore it requires a continuous stimulus for change.

This implies that the function that Plato attributed to art— to stimulate and inspire societal change—is seen by many as essential for continuous development. Since the limit to development, omnicompetence, is an ideal that can never be attained but that can be approached without end, its pursuit should be continuous.

Aristotle's conception of art was very different from Plato's. Plato saw art as inducing change, as a product and producer of *creative* but disruptive acts; Aristotle saw it as retarding change, as a product and producer of *recreative* acts. Aristotle took art to be a cathartic, a palliative for dissatisfaction, hence a producer of stability and contentment. He saw art as something from which one extracts satisfaction here and now.

These apparently contradictory views of art are actually complementary: They are two necessary aspects of ideal-pursuit. The value obtained from recreation is *intrinsic*. it consists of the satisfaction, the *fun and entertainment,* we derive from what we do regardless of what we do it for. It is the satisfaction we derive from "going there" in contrast to the satisfaction derived from "getting there." Recreation provides "the pause that refreshes," thereby re-creating creators. We would not be able to maintain continuous pursuit of ends that cannot be attained without payoffs along the way.

The property of nature and art we call beauty *inspires* us and arouses the courage required to make further progressive efforts. Beauty stimulates visions of things better than what we have and instills in us the desire to pursue them. A sense of making progress toward our ideals is what makes life meaningful; it endows life with *extrinsic* value.

Intrinsic and extrinsic values. We have preferences for means (courses of action) as well as for ends (valued outcomes) because, as I pointed out earlier, ends and means are relative concepts. Every end is a means to a further end, and every means is an end in itself. Therefore, means as well as ends have a value to us. They have two kinds of value: *extrinsic* or *instrumental*, and *intrinsic* or *stylistic*. The extrinsic value of a means is its efficiency for an end; its intrinsic value has to do with the satisfaction we derive from using it that is independent of the outcome it produces, regardless of what it is used for.

For example, purple shoes may be just as efficient for walking as black ones. But most of us prefer one to the other. My preference for black shoes is not based on their efficiency, but on the satisfaction I get from wearing them. Similarly, my preferences for black ink over green, and green over pink, exist even though I am aware of the fact that they work equally well. My preference for one type of music over another has nothing to do with efficiency.

Our preferences for means that are based on their intrinsic value, the satisfaction we derive from using them rather than from the outcomes they produce, constitute our *style*. Our individuality, our uniqueness, lies as much in our style as it does in the ends we pursue and the efficiency with which we pursue them. Style has to do with the satisfaction, the *recreational* value, we derive from what we do rather than what we do it for. Until our theories of decision-making, problem-solving, and management take decision-makers' styles into account, they will be seriously deficient.

With social-systemic thinking has come the realization that

unless the aesthetic values of the employed are taken into account in the workplace, they will not be as productive as they can otherwise be. Aesthetics has to do with the quality of work life, a subject on which the next chapter focuses.

Summary

We looked at enterprises as society might if it conceptualized them as social systems, ones that have responsibilities to the individuals and smaller systems that they contain, the larger systems that contain them, and other systems that this larger system contains. This perspective produces the stakeholder view of the firm, a view that reveals that an enterprise consumes resources and makes consumption possible. The excess of the consumption it makes possible over what it consumes constitutes wealth. Therefore, from society's social-systemic point of view, the principal functions of an enterprise are to create and distribute wealth.

The principal way an enterprise distributes wealth is through employment, the only way known to create and distribute wealth simultaneously. Failure of the private sector to provide enough employment to distribute wealth equitably leads to nationalization of enterprises to maintain or increase employment. Unfortunately, such employment as nationalization usually provides is usually unproductive. Therefore it does not create enough wealth to meet minimal requirements even when equitably distributed. This is reflected in the decline and demise of socialistic and communistic economies.

It is only through growth that an enterprise can simultaneously increase its productivity and maintain or increase employment. Therefore, growth is necessary for an enterprise for several reasons: to survive, let alone thrive, in a competitive global economy; to provide enough productive employment to create wealth; and to distribute that wealth equitably. Therefore, growth of an enterprise should be viewed as a means, not an end. The appropriate end of an enterprise viewed as a social system is development.

Development is an increase in the ability and desire to satisfy one's own needs and legitimate desires, and those of others. Competence is a product of development. The limit to development is omnicompetence: an ability to obtain whatever one wants and needs and to enable others to do the same. Because this is an ideal, it can never be attained, but it can be approached without end. Moreover, it is a meta-ideal, an ideal that, if attained, would assure the attainment of all other ideals.

There are four pursuits necessary for continuous development: the pursuits of truth, plenty, the good, and fun and beauty. These are the domains of science and technology; economic, health, educational, and security-producing institutions; ethics and morality; and aesthetics, respectively. Of these, the last two are the least understood.

Social-systemic ethics clearly have important implications for corporate behavior. First, they imply providing all those who have a stake in corporate decisions with an opportunity to participate directly or indirectly in making them. Second, they require monitoring the decisions made to be sure that future options are not closed but, if anything, are increased. In addition, the decisions should be monitored to determine if they were mistaken; if so, why; and then corrections made—all this to maximize learning. Social-systemic ethics implies the right to make mistakes and to try again. Finally, the young and the yet-to-be-born should have their interests protected by increasing, not foreclosing, the options that will be available to them when they can participate.

Aesthetic activities and products provide the recreative rewards, fun and entertainment, derived from pursuing ideals and relaxing from their pursuit; and the inspiration required to pursue something that can be approached but never attained. Aesthetic values, fun and inspiration, have to do with the quality of our lives. In Part II we look for ways to achieve the kind of organization and management called for by systemic thinking. In Chapter 3 we see how the quality of the work lives of those employed by an enterprise affects the quality of the products and services it provides.

Part *II*

Foreground

This part presents ways of transforming organizations to ones that move beyond merely running to catch up to their competitors to ones that explore new ways of pursuing quality; dealing with the need, and the way, to democratize organizations; and converting their internal economies into market economies. It presents an organizational structure that eliminates what is probably the most debilitating activity that most corporations engage in, reorganization. The multidimensional organization eliminates this need and combines in a very effective way with a democratic internal market economy. It concludes with a new model of management education that will yield leaders equipped to transform their organizations.

Chapter 3

Quality of Work Life and Its Products

The more that corporations think of themselves as social systems—even if they don't use the term themselves—the less they focus on growth for its own sake, and the more they focus on development. The focus of their developmental efforts is on their employees. Of all their stakeholders, employees obviously have the most direct effect on corporate performance. The more corporations focus on the development of their employees, the more they must concern themselves with the quality of the work lives they provide, because their quality of work life is the best index of their work-related development.

As pointed out in Chapter 1, industrializing societies were able to "get away with" dehumanized work as long as it required little skill, workers were poorly educated, and unemployment brought with it a threat of economic destitution. But the Industrial Revolution eventually created wealth, some of which was used to provide workers with greater economic security and more and better education. Secure and educated workers were and are increasingly dissatisfied with machine-like work—short, simple, dull, repetitive tasks. As a result, alienation from work has reached crisis proportions in some advanced industrialized nations.

Industrialization accelerated urbanization, which brought about fundamental qualitative changes in the environments in which people worked and lived. Most of the places in which developed people spend their time are now people-made. Initially, people-made environments brought comfort and convenience, but many of them have been deteriorating rapidly in recent years. This deterioration is exacerbated by decreasing access to untouched Nature. The Industrial Revolution not only led to dissatisfaction with quality of work life, but also with quality of life in general.

Quality of life in general, and quality of work life in particular, are aesthetic considerations, but until very recently aesthetics has been the odd man out in Western development. It is the least understood of the four dimensions of progress toward the ideal of development, omnicompetence. This ideal, it will be recalled, is the ability to satisfy all one's own needs and legitimate desires, and those of others.

Our preoccupation with quality of life, including work life, has been increasing since World War II. The West is gradually becoming aware of the fact that it has been trying to sing four-part harmony with only three voices: scientific-technological, economic, and ethical-moral. Aesthetics has been missing.

The more one's basic needs for food, health, clothing, and shelter are satisfied, the more one becomes concerned with quality of life. Little wonder then that an increasingly educated and economically secure workforce in the West demands a more satisfying quality of work life. Unfortunately, efforts to provide it are hampered by lack of a clear understanding of the nature of "quality of life" and "quality of work life."

In Chapter 2 we saw that our development has less to do with what we have than with how much we can do with whatever we have. We saw that development is best reflected in quality of life. This quality is a matter of aesthetics; it is derived from the satisfaction (fun) we get from doing what we do regardless of what we do it for, and a sense of progress toward the developmental ideal, omnicompetence, the meaningfulness of what we are doing.

The higher our standard of living, the more consideration we give to the fun we derive from what we do and its meaningfulness. For example, the three owners and executives of a very successful but small hand-tool-manufacturing company wanted to diversify so they could become more involved in their business. Their company virtually ran itself, requiring little of their time or attention. Of course, they would like to have increased their profits, but not nearly as much as they wanted to increase the satisfaction they derived from running the business. This was a quality-of-work-life, not a standard-of-living, issue for the owners. They eventually added a new product line that required their intense involvement and their learning a whole new technology. They found the challenge exciting and their reinvolvement in the business a source of great personal satisfaction. All this had an unexpected benefit: The morale and productivity of their employees increased because they saw their bosses working for their living.

A very much larger but equally successful company that dominated its industry began to lose market share because of severe price-cutting by its principal competitors. Its production costs were higher than its competitors' because of its commitment to producing only the highest-quality products. Had it been willing to reduce the quality of its products to that of its competitors, it could easily have been the low-cost producer in the field. This would have made it possible for it to reduce the price its products and maintain, if not increase, its market share. Nevertheless, the company's executives would not reduce the quality of its products because they felt that the satisfaction they and the other employees derived from knowing their products were the best available would be significantly reduced. This potential loss of job satisfaction was worth more to them than the additional profit the company might have made by sacrificing their products' quality. This commitment to product quality clearly had more to do with their quality of life than with their standard of living. It was not long before consumers decided that the quality difference was worth the price difference, and the company not only regained its market share but also gained some.

I once worked with two different districts of the Federal Reserve Bank at the same time. Both had exactly the same functions. Nevertheless, their work environments were completely different. The one conceptualized as a social system operated as a democratic community with a great deal of informal as well as formal participation in decision-making. The other was operated as a machine, a rigid bureaucratic hierarchy in which everyone was bounded and knew what those boundaries were. In the former, employees' morale at all levels was high; they were having fun at work. Although they did not "look" as busy as those in the second bank, they were much more productive. They understood how what they did affected the bank's overall performance, and they focused on improving it. This gave them a feeling that what they were doing was of value to society at large. At the other bank, almost all non-managerial employees were bored, could not see the value of what they were doing, and hence did not feel as though they were part of something of value. The differences between the two banks were almost entirely aesthetic.

The fact that most work is not fun or fulfilling is not surprising, because in the mechanistic and organismic view of work it was not supposed to be either. These properties have relevance only when those at work are treated as purposeful human beings, not as purposeless organs or machine parts. The idea of integrating work, play, and learning is a new one.

The Integration of Work, Play, and Learning

The dominant mode of thought introduced to the Western world during the Renaissance was analytic. In analysis, what we try to understand is first taken apart. Then an effort is made to understand the behavior or properties of its parts taken separately. Finally, this understanding is aggregated in an effort to understand the behavior or properties of the whole. Just about everything that people could think of was subjected to analysis, including life itself. Life was analyzed, decomposed, into three distinct types of activity: work, play, and learning. This separation was deeply rooted in Western cultures. Institutions were devoted to each, but almost always to only one. Factories were designed for work, but excluded the possibility of play and learning. Country clubs, arenas, and stadiums were designed for having fun but not for doing work or learning. Schools were designed for learning but not for work or fun. Human activities directed at work, play, and learning were kept separate physically and in time.

The Industrial Revolution led to the creation of work and workplaces that excluded fun and learning, hence development of the worker. Rationalization of this separation was provided by the "Protestant ethic." This ethic contrasts work and play. It conceptualizes work as necessary and necessarily unpleasant, *ascetically,* not *aesthetically.* This ethic asserts that the dissatisfaction work produces should be accepted, if not embraced, as an earthly purgatory in which sin is expiated and virtue is gradually accumulated. Work was thought of as a type of punishment, not as an opportunity for self-fulfillment and pleasure. Some even thought the displeasure associated with work was good for the soul; the greater the displeasure, the more it cleansed the soul.

This is no longer the prevailing view of work. Today we increasingly believe that everyone is entitled to work that not only satisfies but also that contributes to the development of the worker. The test for determining the extent to which these conditions are met reveals clearly what the objective of work design should be. The test consists of posing the following question: *Suppose you are told right now that you will continue to draw your current salary in constant dollars for the rest of your life and you need not work anymore to receive it. What would you do tomorrow?* If the answer is anything but "I would come back to work tomorrow and do exactly what I am doing today," the quality of work life needs improvement.

The higher the quality of work life the producers of products or services enjoy, the higher the quality of products or services they produce. These two types of quality are closely related. Those who do not enjoy a high quality of work life transform their dissatisfaction with their work into the poor quality of products or services they produce. The current plethora of programs to increase quality of outputs cannot succeed unless the quality of the input, the work life that went into them, is also high. Treating the quality of outputs (products and services) independently of the quality of inputs (work life) is bound to fail in the long run, if not the short run. In this chapter I will also consider how to tie these two types of quality together so that employee, customer, and consumer satisfaction are inextricably united.

Quality of Life

In the previous chapter I argued that decision-making has two important aesthetic aspects. First, there is the *style* of decision-makers, their preferences that have nothing to do with the efficiency of what they do, but with the satisfaction they derive from doing it. Second, there is the sense of progress they derive from moving toward their developmental ideal—the perceived meaningfulness of what they do. Unless we understand the roles of style and a sense of progress toward ideals in decision-making, we cannot deal effectively with quality-of-life problems.

One source of the current concern of some people with quality of life is the fact that they derive decreasing satisfaction from the ordinary things they do such as taking a walk, an automobile ride on Sunday, attending school, going to work, and so on. To be sure, people have been saying "things are getting worse" since at least the dawn of recorded history. But there are types of deterioration currently taking place that have no precedent—for example, the spread and pervasiveness of graffiti, crime, drug addiction, litter, air and water pollution, one-parent families, homelessness, and traffic congestion. These conditions reduce the amount of fun that many derive from ordinary things they do or want to do. Reduction of the quality of work life is a special case of the dissatisfaction produced by the lack of intrinsic value (fun) to be found in the work environment and the work done in it.

The second aspect of reduced quality of life derives from the growing feeling that much of our increasingly rapid cultural, social, economic, and technological change is "getting us nowhere." Inspiring leadership and ideas seem to be less pervasive. There are few mobilizing causes and movements gripping large numbers of people. The radical "idealism" of the post-World War II era has settled down to the conservative "realism" of the past two decades. This means that there is little or no sense of progress toward such ideals as peace on Earth, peace of mind, equality of opportunity, financial security, and elimination of poverty. A sense of progress toward ideals gives life meaning, makes choice significant. However, today many feel that they have little real choice, no control over their futures. They are driven to fatalism, resignation to a future that they believe is determined by the past rather than by what they do. All this reduces the quality of life.

Measuring Quality of Life

How do we know that quality of life is deteriorating? Can this quality be measured? If not, does this mean that discussion of it is not useful?

Measurement of an individual's and a society's quality of life is very difficult, if at all possible. Because of this difficulty, considerable effort has been devoted to developing social indicators of it. Unfortunately, use of such indicators raises a fundamental methodological problem. Their usefulness and appropriateness depend on how well they correlate with the measure of quality of life for which they are substitutes. Since we do not have such a measure of quality of life with which to compare these indices, we cannot evaluate them objectively. Therefore, attempts have been made to correlate social indicators with qualitative evaluations of the quality of life. But this raises another set of methodological questions: Whose evaluation should be used? Made where and when? What confidence can be placed in these evaluations? Finally and most critically: Why not use qualitative evaluations directly, without indicators?

There is a certain attractiveness in the argument that qualitative judgments of the quality of life are good enough for our purposes. The quality of life is so poor for some segments of society that even crude judgments are more than satisfactory for most purposes. The same can be said of those situations in which the quality of life is extremely good.

But how can a person judge the effects of his or her actions on another person's quality of life when the effects are relatively small but significant? One person cannot know all the relevant values of another; there are too many of them. In addition, these preferences change over time and from environment to environment.

Qualitative judgments of another's quality of life may enable us to identify some of the larger problems to be solved, but they are not always good enough to determine how best to solve them. More precise judgments than most of us can make about another's quality of life seem to be required to determine how to make even incremental improvements in their quality of life.

Must we wait until an ability to measure quality of life easily is developed before designers, planners, and managers of social systems can effectively improve it? Must we go ahead without the precision and accuracy of judgment that seem to be required to plan effectively for improvement of another's quality of life? Or is there an alternative approach that does not require our making such evaluations but that yields effective solutions to quality-of-life problems? There is such an approach, but it requires a radical change in how decisions affecting the quality of life of others are made.

An Alternative Approach to Quality-of-Life Problems

Because individuals whose quality of life is poor can seldom do much to improve it, well-meaning social planners, politicians, and managers often try to do something to and for them. As we have seen, these do-gooders are handicapped by an inability to evaluate precisely the quality they try to improve. However, if those whose quality of life is involved were given an opportunity to affect that quality significantly, there would be no need for others to try to do it for them. *People who can make quality-of-life decisions for themselves have less of an evaluative problem than others who try to make these decisions for them.*

Once planners and managers give up the idea of redesigning the work of others and, instead, give them an opportunity to design their own work and work environment, they have no difficulty in bringing about changes that lead to significant improvements in their quality of work life. Workers are more likely than planners or managers to know what dissatisfies them, what causes these dissatisfactions, and what to do about them. To be sure, if workers are in control of the nature of their work, they are more likely to recognize and correct their mistakes than are managers and planners likely to recognize and correct theirs.

It has long been known that participation in making quality-of-work-life decisions leads to significant improvements in that quality. For example, according to Paul Blumberg (1969), a widely recognized authority on this subject: "There is hardly a study in the entire literature which fails to demonstrate that satisfaction in work is enhanced or that other generally acknowledged beneficial consequences accrue, from a general increase in workers' decision-making power. Such consistency of findings, I submit, is rare in social research" (p. 123).

Although redesigning one's own work does not require measurement of the quality of work life that results, it would be foolish to say that it could not benefit from such measurement. Of course it could. But experience with participative design has shown that it produces greater increases in satisfaction with work than redesign by others regardless of the measures and indices with which the others are equipped. The reason is clear: *Participation*, which is a form of self-determination, *is itself a major source of satisfaction* and therefore of improved quality of life. It has considerable intrinsic as well as extrinsic value. Put another way: Participation in the redesign of one's own work not only has improved quality of work life as its product, but also itself enhances the quality of work life—that is, has intrinsic as well as extrinsic value.

For these reasons we should not focus on the question, How can we improve the quality of (work) life of others? but on the question, *How can we enable others to improve their own quality of (work) life?* This reformulated problem does not require measures or precise judgments of the quality of (work) life of others for its solution. However, it does require unconventional concepts of participation and design, ones in which the ethics and aesthetics of the participants play a major role.

This results in the convergence of ethics and aesthetics, the integration of both types of value.

Interactive idealized design. Participants in design processes cannot help but put their ethical and aesthetic values into the designs they produce. How much of their values they insert depends on how constrained the design process is. The less constrained the process, the more of their values that find their way into the design. The *interactive idealized design process* imposes very few constraints on those who participate in it.

There are two types of idealized design: bounded and unbounded. A bounded idealized design of a system, social or otherwise, begins with the assumption that the system involved was destroyed last night. It no longer exists, but its environment is assumed to remain as it was, untouched. If the redesigned organization is part of a corporation—for example, a division or a department—this means that the rest of the corporation is initially assumed to remain as it was; only the unit involved is assumed to have been destroyed.

Assuming destruction of an existing organization, the participants design the system—for example, enterprise or government—they would ideally have right now if they could have whatever organization they wanted. This design should be subject to only three requirements.

First, the design must be *technologically feasible*. The intent of this requirement is to prevent the design from being a work of science fiction. For example, one cannot assume the availability of a way of directly transferring the content of one mind to another by telepathy or of moving people by use of such a transporter as appears on *Star Trek*. It is important to note that this requirement does not preclude technological innovation—for example, invention of the fax machine or the videophone. There is no requirement that the design or any of its parts be economically feasible.

However, the second requirement is that the design must

be *operationally viable,* capable of working and surviving in the current environment *if* it were brought into existence. However, it need not be capable of being implemented. This removes the need to consider its practicality but it does require that the system designed obeys relevant laws and regulations currently enforced.

Third, because any design is unintentionally but inevitably constrained by the designers' lack of at least some relevant information, knowledge, understanding, and wisdom, the system designed should be *capable of learning* from its own experience *and adapting* to internal and external changes. It should also be subject to change by internal and external agents. In other words, it should be ready, willing, and able continuously to improve itself and be improved by others.

An idealized design is neither ideal nor utopian because it is capable of improvement. It is the best (virtually unconstrained) design its designers can prepare now, but its design, unlike that of a utopia, is based on the assumption that nothing real can remain even approximately ideal for long. Therefore, the term "idealized' refers to the fact that the design is the best *ideal-seeking system* its designers can produce now.

In an unbounded idealized design of a system, the designers are permitted to change any of the containing systems, but only in ways that affect the performance of the system involved. For example, in such a design a division of a corporation could change the restrictive hiring practices of the corporation of which it is part, or it might relax the requirement that it be supplied with parts by an internal rather than an external supplier.

The idealized design process provides an effective way of obtaining meaningful participation of all the system's current stakeholders or their representatives. It facilitates participation because it is *fun* and it requires no special skills to be able to engage in and contribute to it. Most disagreements about a design arise from consideration of efficiency, not value. Since idealized design is preoccupied with value, not efficiency, it tends to generate consensus among those participating in it.

Consensus designs. Decisions made by a majority of participants usually create a dissatisfied minority. Most tyrannies are tyrannies of a minority by a majority. Decision-making by consensus avoids such abuse, but it appears to make reaching a conclusion very difficult if not impossible. This only *appears* to be the case because the nature of consensus is not well understood. It is complete agreement, not in principle, but *in practice.* It is this distinction that is not widely grasped.

Consider an example: In one corporation a large number of managers was divided into eight groups, each of which was asked independently to prepare an idealized redesign of their company. When all had completed this task, they assembled and presented their designs to the others. When the chief executive officer asked for an expression of opinion to determine which of the eight designs was preferred, he received about a one-eighth vote for each. He turned to me in desperation saying that he could not get a majority let alone complete agreement, and asked what he should do. I told him that I thought he had consensus even if he did not have a majority. He looked at me with surprise and asked where I had been during the vote he had just taken. I told I had been listening but that I had heard something other than what he had heard. I asked for the floor and gave the assemblage the following choice: keep the current organization without change, or allow me to pick one of the eight designs at random. There was a unanimous vote in favor of my making the random choice. (It was not necessary for me to make one because the groups went back to work and came up with a design that all agreed should be implemented.) *Agreement in practice is agreement to act; it does not require that the approved action is taken by all to be the best in principle.*

In group design processes consensus on most design decisions is reached without any special effort. When consensus is not reached, an attempt should first be made to design a test of the alternatives proposed, a test that all the participants accept as fair and one by whose outcome they are willing to abide. For example, in one company, agreement could not be reached as to whether the plant-maintenance department in a multiplant operation should be placed under a plant manager or a functional manager of engineering located at corporate headquarters. A multiplant test was designed that all the participants considered to be fair. The test was conducted, and the findings were accepted and implemented without complaint. It turned out that the best arrangement depended on plant characteristics. Therefore, in some of the plants the maintenance department reported to the plant manager, in others to the corporate head of engineering.

In most cases, preferences and differences of opinion are based on different beliefs concerning a question of fact. The critical fact in the plant-maintenance case was about the relative efficiency and responsiveness of maintenance personnel under two different organizational arrangements. It is much easier to design a test of a question of fact than one of value.

The most dramatic case of differing opinions that I have experienced involved a small Indian village in a very remote part of Mexico. The community could not agree on whether to use capital punishment for capital crimes. Some argued that such punishment was necessary to deter capital crimes; others argued that it had no such effect and often resulted in killing innocent people. Therefore, the difference in attitudes was based on a difference of opinion about a question of fact. Does capital punishment deter capital crimes? A retrospective experiment was designed in which there was no need to kill anyone. All those in the town meeting approved of the test and committed themselves to abide by its outcome.

The states in Mexico were divided into four categories: (1) those that did not have capital punishment five years ago and still did not have it; (2) those that had capital punishment five years ago and still had it; (3) those that had it five years ago but discontinued it in the past five years; and (4) those that did not have it five years ago but introduced it in the past five years. By comparing the changes in the number of capital crimes in each category it was possible to determine whether capital punishment had had any deterrent effect.

When completed, the test revealed that the number of capital crimes in Mexico was not reduced by capital punishment. The community illegalized capital punishment.

In some cases there is either not enough time to design and conduct an acceptable test, or resolution of the issue involved does not justify the cost of a test. When it is apparent that consensus cannot be reached through discussion and a test is not feasible or practical, the chairperson should go around the room asking participants to state their positions succinctly. Then the chairperson should reveal his or her choice. However, if the others reach agreement, even if it differs from the the chairperson's intentions, the chairperson will accept it and act accordingly. Then the chairperson goes around the room once again asking for each participant's opinion. If two or more participants disagree, then they agree in effect on the chairperson's choice.

In the many participative design sessions of which I have been a part, I have never experienced one in which consensus could not be reached by one of these three procedures. With experience it becomes progressively easier to attain.

Planning implementation of the design.   Once an idealized design is completed, plans can be made to approximate it as closely as possible. Once the means for doing so have been selected, the resource they require can be determined and planned for. If the resources required cannot be obtained, the approximation to the idealized design that had been settled on earlier may have to be "taken down a notch or two." If more resources will be available than are required, either the requirements should be "taken up a notch," or excess resources should be disposed of in some productive way. Then it is necessary to determine who is going to do what, where, and when. Finally, it is necessary to select ways of monitoring and evaluating the implementation, and correcting the design or its implementation when either fails to meet or exceed expectations.

The process just described is a very much abbreviated version of *interactive planning*. A much more detailed discussion is provided in Ackoff (1981).

Despite the apparent desirability of quality-of-work-life programs, they have not become as pervasive in the past four decades as many thought and hoped they would (Trist, 1981). Speaking of the first international Quality-of-Working-Life (QWL) conference, held in Toronto in 1972, Will McWhinney (1992) wrote:

> Not all employees and rather few managers would participate in humanistic approaches to designing their environments, and in only a few companies and communities would workers or residents come to control significant resources and opportunities. Limitations became apparent, and skeptical queries or outright opposition came from all sides . . . It was obviously easier to start prototypes than to propagate them. Regressions have been more common than sustained changes. . . .
>
> Some industrial organizations and community projects that have approached social change through concepts of network formation (for examples, see Trist, 1985) and organizational transformation (Levy & Merry, 1986) have shown vitality and reproducibility. Yet the slowly increasing rate of success is not sufficient to establish that a "paradigm change" has taken place. [p. 6]

Avoiding Failure of Quality-of-Work-Life Programs

Why has the QWL movement stalled? There are a number of reasons, any one of which would probably have been enough to stunt its growth. However, I believe they reduce to one general and pervasive deficiency: *In the work involved in designing,*

installing, and operating most QWL programs, their proponents
have failed to apply one or more of the principles they try to apply
to the work of others. In examining these principles it should be
borne in mind that all QWL programs involve the formation of
groups that have at least some control over the quality of the
work life of their members. How these groups should be
formed and how they should operate are discussed in Chapter
4. The principles are as follows:

1. All those who can be directly affected by a QWL program should participate in its design, implementation, and
   operation. This implies that the quality of the work life of
   managers at all levels should be improved before or while the
   quality of the work life of nonmanagerial personnel is dealt
   with.

Where this is not done, managers, particularly those at middle
and lower levels, often obstruct or sabotage the QWL effort. In
my experience it has been just such obstruction that is the
principal reason for the failure or disappointing results of
QWL efforts.

Managers are also people with purposes of their own.
Their quality of work life is often worse than that of production
workers. Therefore, their resentment of the workplace and the
boss can be even more intense than that of lower-level employees. Moreover, they may well feel less secure in their jobs
than any other employees because contraction of middle managers has been greater than at any other organizational level. If
they feel they have been overlooked, they will try to see to it that
no one else gets the attention they feel they deserve.

On the other hand, participation in these programs should
not be voluntary for managers at any level; their participation
should be a condition of their employment.

2. Once managers are taken care of, the quality-of-work-life
   program should be extended to cover all white-, gray-, and
   blue-collar workers.

If any group of participants is omitted. they will resent it and are likely to obstruct implementation of the program. White-collar workers are even more commonly omitted than middle managers. Yet white-collar workers are more numerous in most companies than blue-collar workers.

Participation by nonmanagerial personnel should be voluntary. Their voluntary participation is an indication of the value of the program to them and therefore, provides important feedback. A program that starts with less than complete participation—and most do—can use the increase/decrease in participation as a very important measure of its success/failure.

> 3. Managers and workers should be prepared for these programs by receiving instruction in cooperative group processes, and attendees at these sessions should not be homogeneous with respect to status. Each class should be a cross section of the workforce.

Effective groups seldom come about spontaneously. Few people know how to work well in groups. Classes that are homogeneous with respect to status and rank reinforce hierarchy and undermine the effort to democratize. Different levels have to learn how to interact effectively, and there is no better place for this to begin that where they are instructed on how to work in heterogeneous groups.

When unions are involved, their officers should be invited to participate in the program. Union officials will seldom support a QWL program in which they do not play a central role. They generally see such programs as efforts to undermine their influence over the workforce. It is only by involving them and giving them a voice in the design and conduct of the program that their fear can be allayed.

Furthermore, lower-level employees are wary of experts, especially those employed by management, and suspect that programs designed by such experts are instruments of subtle exploitation. Unfortunately, their suspicion is often justified. Therefore, participation by union officials gives them some assurance that they are not being deceived.

4. Once the programs are initiated, efforts should be made to correct undesirable behavior in the workplace rather than punish those responsible for it and try to make an example of them. Problem people should be made the responsibility of their peers, not their superiors.

Punishment seldom produces lasting good behavior, and even less frequently produces a satisfied worker or manager.

5. Corrective action applied to those who break the rules should be determined and applied regardless of rank.

There should not be double standards; responses to recalcitrant managers should be the same as those applied to recalcitrant nonmanagerial personnel.

6. Commitments to do something made by any participant in a quality-of-work-life program should be monitored and met.

If a participant cannot meet a commitment, a complete explanation of the failure should be given to those who are directly affected, and the responsibility should be reassigned.

7. Quality-of-work-life meetings should not be permitted to break up into caucus meetings.

Caucuses preserve adversarial relationships and convert quality-of-work-life meetings into negotiating, rather than co-operative, sessions. To the extent possible, all discussion should take place openly in meetings attended by both parties. It takes a while for people to become comfortable talking frankly in the presence of those they once considered adversaries, but how long it takes depends on how much practice they get.

> 8. An experienced and competent third party should be engaged initially to facilitate joint meetings of normally conflicting parties until they can run themselves.

Selection of the third party should be subject to approval by the principal parties and be dismissible by any one of them.

The Payoff of QWL

The QWL movement has not died, but it is in a coma. It can be revitalized. I believe this can be done by engaging the workforce in the idealized redesign of its work and workplace, and subsequently in implementing as close an approximation to its design as is possible. This happened at Alcoa's Tennessee operations.

Alcoa Tennessee. In 1983, Dick Ray, the manager of these Operations, and Tim Garner, then head of Local 309 of the United Steel Workers, which represented the Operation's hourly-paid workers, appeared together on a platform to discuss the QWL program they had jointly initiated in 1980. They were asked what had been the principal effect of the program on them personally. They looked at each other, smiled, and said this was a question they had discussed between themselves many times. The answer was simple: They now looked forward to coming to work in the morning, whereas they had once dreaded it. Work was now *fun*. Moreover, it was *meaningful:* They had changed the mind of Alcoa executives who, before initiation of the QWL program, had decided to shut down the Operations because of its low productivity and poor quality of product. These performance characteristics had so improved since initiation of the program that the parent company was now committed not only to keeping the Operations going but also to investing a great deal of money in modernizing the old plants. The QWL program had saved thousands of jobs and now provided them with an opportunity to apply more technology to their work than had ever previously been attempted. This, they said, was a consequence of the preparation of an idealized redesign of the Operations in which they and employees at all levels of the organization had been engaged. Its approximation presented an exciting challenge to all. To carry out that approximation would require learning a great deal; this was the exciting challenge.

On October 23, 1987, the most advanced aluminum cold mill in the world was dedicated at Alcoa Tennessee.

Shortly after the QWL program was introduced, two of the hourly-paid workers stationed at the end of an aluminum sheet rolling mill made a change in their work that saved the company a great deal of money. When I heard about this I went down to congratulate them. They were proud as punch. After the praise I asked them how long they had known about the possible improvement. They both looked down and did not answer. I pressed. Finally, without looking up, one mumbled, "fifteen years." I was surprised and asked why they had waited so long to implement their idea. One of them looked up and said, "Those sons of bitches never asked us before."

These two incidents exemplify the aspirations of QWL programs. They are intended to make work fun and meaningful, and to give those at work the opportunity to use what they know and to learn new things.

Alcoa Tennessee showed how a quality-of-work-life program can save even an organization bound for closure. Such programs have done more than that; they have also brought back to life enterprises that have died. The following is such a case.

Super Fresh. A&P closed 2,500 of its stores, 79 in the Philadelphia area, between 1974 and 1982. At the instigation of Local 1357 of the United Food and Commercial Workers, which had lost thousands of its members as a result of these closings, a study was initiated to determine whether their closed stored could be resurrected profitably. A team consisting of A&P managers, officers of the local, a number of workers who had lost their jobs, and members of the Busch Center of The Wharton School produced an idealized redesign of a supermarket chain that all members of the team considered to be a viable alternative to the stores that had been closed. By mutual agreement these stores were remodeled and reopened as part of a new subsidiary of A&P called Super Fresh.

The major differences from the old stores were the design of work and the work environment. To use a currently popular term, the workers were greatly empowered. The changed relationship between management and labor was reflected in an interview of Gerald Goode, the first president of Super Fresh (*The Wall Street Journal,* September 29, 1983), who said the stores no longer had employees, only "associates."

In the last five months of 1982, twenty four stores were reopened and 2,105 people returned to work. On April 3, 1983, a local paper, *The Philadelphia Inquirer,* reported: "[W]hile competitors complain, Super Fresh continues to open stores at such a rapid clip that it is beginning to run out of prime locations. As of this week, 45 of the 79 area markets that once were A&P stores have reopened as Super Fresh markets and eight to 12 more are expected to be opened by July 1."

Super Fresh continues to operate successfully and expand today. Jamshid Gharajedaghi, then an adjunct professor at Wharton and now president of the Institute for Interactive Management, and who guided Super Fresh through its resurrection, continues to shepherd its development and growth. In an earlier description of this case I wrote:

> The resurrection of A&P as Super Fresh suggests, first, new collaborative and entrepreneurial roles for unions in revitalization of dying or dead businesses; second, that managers are

learning how to make better use of the knowledge and good will of their workers; and, finally, that third parties can enable two parties locked in mortal combat to find creative win-win ways of dissolving their differences. [Ackoff, 1986, p. 56]

The 1950–60 preoccupation of corporations with quality of work life shifted in the 1980s to quality of the products or services provided to customers. These two quality-related movements are not as disconnected as may appear.

Total Quality Management (TQM)

Following the Japanese, total quality management (TQM) is currently a very popular means by which American management is trying to pursue improvement of corporate performance and competitiveness in the global economy. This popularity is reflected in the television programs, videotapes, and book written by Lloyd Dobyns and Clare Crawford-Mason (1991). A good deal of this popularity stems from the fact that the TQM movement is believed to have originated in the work of the Americans W. Edwards Deming (1986), Philip B. Crosby (1979), J. R. Juran (1989), and Armand V. Feigenbaum (1990).

The enthusiasm that TQM currently engenders in managerial circles may not be justified. From a survey of 500 executives conducted by Opinion Research Corporation for Arthur D. Little (1992), Dr. P. Ranganath Nayak, a senior vice president of Arthur D. Little, concluded that

[T]raining employees in problem-solving and empowering them to find localized, incremental solutions—the essence of today's Total Quality Management (TQM) movement—in and of itself won't result in the significant improvement needed to become what he and his colleagues refer to as high-performance businesses.

"A high-performance business," he explains, "is a world-class organization that is able to improve faster than the competition and sustain that higher rate indefinitely. [p. 1]

This conclusion is echoed by one obtained from a study of 584 companies in the United States, Canada, Germany, and Japan; the study was conducted by Ernst and Young for the American Quality Foundation. The October 1, 1992, issue of *The Wall Street Journal* reported:

> The study, released today, raises striking doubts about several trendy practices that comprise the growing "total quality movement—such as worker teams and "benchmarking," or emulating the best ideas of top companies. Many businesses may waste millions of dollars a year on quality-improvement strategies that don't improve their performance and may even hamper it, the report suggests.

Consider some of the problems associated with TQM.

The Meaning of "Quality"

"Quality" in the TQM context is applied to products or services and has come to be generally accepted as meaning "meeting or exceeding the expectations of customers." Sometimes "at lowest cost, on time, every time" is added. Those who so define quality usually assume that the customers are the same as the consumers. However, this is often *not* the case—for example, where a supplier sells a product to a wholesaler who sells it to a retailer who sells it to someone who may give it as a gift to another. In some cases the customer and the consumer may be the same person or organization, but they need not be. In such cases, most would agree that that quality should be at least as much concerned with the consumers' expectations as the customers'. Since the expectations of customers and consumers are likely to be very different, the distinction between them is critical.

Increasingly, internal consumers of internally provided goods and services are also being taken into account in TQM programs. For example, the "miracle" produced by Jan Carlzon (1987), then CEO of Scandinavian Airlines, is attributed to his making *all* of that airline's employees aware that they had consumers of their outputs and that they were responsible for meeting or exceeding their consumers' expectations. Aircraft-maintenance personnel are the customers of those who operate the tool room and parts supply. Agents are the customers of those who operate the computerized reservation system.

The concept of "consumer" has been enlarged over time and, as it has, the field on which quality has focused has become larger. It has become increasingly *total*, but in most cases not total enough. Total quality should apply to the expectations of all those who are affected by what an organization does, all its stakeholders. This means meeting the expectations of an organization's suppliers, employees, consultants and advisers, wholesalers, retailers, stockholders, bondholders, bankers, debtors, and so on. Only when it consciously tries to meet all these requirements does it deserve to call its quality program "total."

According to the *Merriam-Webster's Colligiate Dictionary* previously cited, "expect" has two significantly different meanings: (1) "to consider reasonable, due, or necessary" and (2) "to anticipate or look forward to the coming or occurrence of." It is in the first sense, not the second, that quality is defined with reference to the expectations of stakeholders. In this sense, expectations have to do with desires, not forecasts.

TQM is obviously concerned with providing ultimate users of a product or service with the quality they desire at as low a price as possible. Although TQM correctly defines product/service quality in terms of ultimate users' expectations, *it provides no effective way of determining what these expectations are*. Amanda Bennett (1990), writing in *The Wall Street*

Journal, observed that "a growing number of companies are finding out that giving customers what they want isn't nearly as hard as finding out what it is they want." (p. B1). Most quality managers rely on conventional types of marketing research in which consumers are generally asked by means of an oral or written questionnaire to express their preferences, needs, and wants.

This way of determining what consumers want is notoriously inaccurate and unreliable. The respondents are often not aware of what they want, and even if they are, they may be more interested in giving the inquirer answers that they, the consumers, think the inquirers want than in probing their own preferences. When consumers are aware of what they want and are willing to reveal it, their responses to inquiries are likely to be strongly influenced by what is available. They are not likely to reveal needs and desires that they think, often incorrectly, cannot be satisfied.

* Determining what consumers want is seen by those who supply them as increasingly critical because, among other things, product quality is increasingly understood in terms of consumer wants rather than supplier beliefs about what consumers want; and new possibilities for successful product development are increasingly thought to be based on perceptions of unsatisfied consumer needs and desires, even when the consumer is not conscious of them.

* Therefore it is very desirable to have a way of enabling consumers to become aware of what they want and to reveal it as truthfully as they can. Consumer idealized design is such a way.

Consumer Idealized Design (CID)

In CID actual or potential consumers prepare an idealized design of the product or service of interest. It has been applied to such diverse products and services as supermarkets, roofing materials, home furnishing stores, and men's clothing stores.

Men's clothing stores. A chain of men's stores that offered high-quality clothing at discount prices failed to attract affluent, upscale customers. Instead, it attracted bargain hunters from lower-income segments of the population. Repeated questionnaires addressed to potential customers of the type the firm wanted yielded responses that, when used, failed to attract them.

Fifteen representatives of the targeted customer population were invited to spend a Saturday with the university-based research group of which I was a part, designing their ideal men's clothing store. The identity of the sponsor was not revealed, but three of the chain's executives whose affiliation was also not revealed were passive participants.

When the design was completed, the identity of the sponsor was revealed. The team members were then asked to compare the sponsor's stores with the idealized design. The differences cited were large but had not been revealed by any of the previous questionnaires. Here are a few of them.

First, the team members said that they always decided how much to spend for the articles of clothing they wanted before they went shopping. Therefore, they wanted a store that offered the highest quality at their predetermined price, not the lowest price for a predetermined quality. To them, discount prices at any price level implied low quality.

Second, they disliked shopping and tried to minimize it by shopping for several articles at once. Therefore they wanted different articles of clothing of the same size to be grouped together in a store so they could get all they wanted at one place, dealing with only one salesperson. They did not want grouping by type of clothing, which required their hunting all over the store and dealing with multiple personnel.

Third, they wanted the help of salespersons only when

they asked for it. They suggested installing call buttons such as airlines have. They also suggested women as salesclerks because they had more faith in a woman's opinion of their appearance than a man's.

The chain subsequently incorporated some of the design features generated by this exercise in new stores, with noticeable desired effect on the clientele they attracted.

Roofing material. A manufacturer of roofing material for houses was attracted to the idea of consumer design and asked a university-based research group to set up such an exercise. The research group found that there can be as many as five different types of customer for such roofing material. There are the architects who often specify the material to be used, although they neither buy nor ultimately use it; then the local material supply houses, the general contractors, roofing contractors, and the owners of the house. Therefore, five separate design groups were formed, and they were brought into a specially constructed laboratory where they could actually build a portion of a roof with real materials.

The plan was for each subject to design two roofs and then compare and discuss all the designs that members of their group prepared. In all five groups the participants refused to stop with two designs; most continued to work, designing four or five roofs, staying well beyond the time planned.

Four of the five groups designed roofs that were inconsistent with an assumption made by all roofing-material manufacturers—that the roof of a house should look like it is made of either wood or slate shingles, or clay tiles. Most of the roofs designed in this exercise resembled none of these. Rather than flat, repetitive patterns, their roofs had designs on them, some very much like Mondrian paintings. This has led not only to consideration of a completely new type of product line but also consideration of a new way of selling roofing by enabling potential customers to build portions of roofs until they find the one they want.

Idealized design by consumers not only makes producers aware of what consumers expect but also can make the consumers conscious of what they expect.

Du Pont. There are times when consumers cannot articulate their expectations even when participating in an idealized design process. Sometimes they must first experience the product or service they thought would meet their expectations. When they do, they often discover they were wrong. For example, Du Pont Fibers Division often finds that when companies that produce carpeting or rugs receive material that meets their specifications, they find it deficient in ways they had not previously considered. They and Du Pont then often engage in a sequence of trials and errors before they obtain a product that satisfies the floor-covering producer.

Amanda Bennett (1990) noted, "Even after companies figure out what customers want, it's subject to change. . . . In 1985, responding quickly to emergency requests was high on [one company's] customers' wish list. Today it's just part of what is expected" [p. B4].

Continuous Improvement

Continuous-improvement programs are an important part of TQM. They usually begin by examining a current activity, process, product, or service and determining what is wrong with it. Then they focus on opportunities for improving such things as clerical errors, product defects and rejects, and late or incorrect deliveries. To a very large extent, improvement consists of the removal of defects or deficiencies. Therefore, continuous improvement is intended to move products or services incrementally from where they are to where one wants them to be.

There is no doubt that in some situations continuous improvement does lead to better products and services. However, in a significant number of situations, it doesn't. *Defect and deficiency removal provides no assurance of attaining something that is more desirable than what is left behind.* For example, if I turn on a television set in the middle of a weekday, there is very little probability that I will get a program I want. However, it is easy to get rid of such a "defect" by changing the channel. Unfortunately, when I do so I am very likely to get another program I don't want, and I may even get one I want less than the first. The solution to a problem conceptualized as defect removal may be worse than the defect it removes.

Recall what happened in the United States when it tried to get rid of alcoholism by eliminating what it took to be its cause, alcohol. Prohibition did not eliminate alcohol or alcoholism, but it did produce large-scale organized crime. Similarly, in the 1960s, the United States tried to eliminate drug addiction by making illegal all addictive drugs. Again, this "solution" intensified the crime problem and, if anything, encouraged use of addictive drugs. (It reinforced a common desire among drug users to "thumb their nose" at the society from which they are alienated.)

Efforts to decrease crime by putting criminals behind bars fare no better. Studies have shown that those who have spent time in prison are more likely to commit crimes when they come out than they were before they went in. The United States' inclination to imprison criminals is responsible for the fact that it has both a higher percentage of its population in prison than any other country, and the highest crime rate.

The moral of all this is that improvement programs should be directed at getting what people want, not, as is usually the case, at getting rid of what they do not want . This is why idealized design can be very effectively used as the foundation of improvement programs—to define what is wanted and to enable those who change products or processes that they are moving closer to something better than what they are leaving behind.

Discontinuous improvement. Continuous improvement involves relatively small changes made close together in time. If all of a workforce's efforts go into making such changes, it precludes creative leaps. Creative leaps are *discontinuities*, qualitative changes. They involve three steps: identification of self-imposed constraints (assumptions); removing them; and exploring the consequences of their removal. This is why there is always an element of surprise when we are exposed to creative work—it always embodies the denial of something we have taken for granted, usually unconsciously. This is particularly true when we are exposed to the solution of a puzzle that we have not been able to solve. A puzzle is a problem that we cannot solve precisely because of a self-imposed constraint; hence the *aha!* experience when the solution is shown to us.

The point is that *creative but discontinuous improvements* are usually worth much more than a string of *small but continuous improvements*. This is not to say that continuous improvement has no value, but that it can seldom elevate an organization into a leadership position. It should be used to augment, not to substitute for, a discontinuous improvement program.

Creativity is difficult to create, but it can be enhanced where it already exists, and it exists in a suppressed state in most people (witness the creativity widespread among children). There are a number of techniques for stimulating creativity—for example, synectics, brainstorming, TKJ, conceptual blockbusting, and idealized design. Elsa Vergara compared these techniques experimentally and found that idealized design stimulates significantly more creativity than the other techniques available (Ackoff and Vergara, 1981). Recall that idealized design involves starting with the assumption that the thing to be improved was destroyed last night. This assumption leads to the identification and removal of many self-imposed constraints and thereby frees minds to be creative.

Put another way: Continuous improvement, valuable as it is when it does yield improvements, is at best a way of trying to catch up with a leader, Japanese or other. Creative leaps are required to take the lead.

Piecemeal vs. systemic improvement. In continuous improvement, defects in different parts of an organization are often observed independently of each other and therefore are addressed separately. This flies in the face of an important systems principle discussed earlier: *The performance of a system depends on how its parts interact, not on how they act taken separately*. Therefore, when the performances of parts taken separately are improved, it does not follow that the performance of the system as a whole will improve. In fact, in many cases it will get worse. Recall that the best available of each part required for an automobile cannot be assembled into an automobile because they do not fit together. The properties to be desired of the parts of a system should be derived from the properties desired of the whole, not conversely.

This is another reason for initiating a quality program with an idealized design of the system involved: It deals with the whole first, then derives properties of the parts from those of the whole.

Planning Backward

TQM programs focus on trying to go from where one is to where one wants to go. This is not nearly as effective as working backward from where one wants to be to where one is. Working backward simplifies the process of getting what we want, provides greater assurance of getting it, and expands the designers' conception of what is feasible.

It is easier to find a way to get back to where one is from where one wants to be than to find a way from where one is to where one wants to be. Although most adults find this difficult to believe, children don't. Many of them have discovered that it is much easier to find a path through a maze by working from the exit to the entrance than from the entrance to the exit. Professor Richard Bellman of the University of Southern California (1952) found that working backward could be used to solve previously difficult- or impossible-to-solve mathematical problems in which the origin and destination were known, but how to get from one to the other was not. He called the procedure dynamic programming.

The working-backward principle is not obvious, but the simple algebraic example given in the Appendix not only shows that it is true but also why.

Working backward from the present. Most continuous-improvement programs, like most strategic plans, work from where one is to where one wants to be at some *future* time, whereas those engaged in idealized design and interactive planning (Ackoff, 1981) work backward from *where one wants to be right now* to *where one is right now*. The reason is that unless one knows where one wants to be right now, how can one possibly know where one will want to be at some time in a future at least some of whose important characteristics cannot be predicted? Furthermore, where we currently think we will want to be in the future is usually very different from where we will want to be in the future. We and our environments change in unpredictable ways between now and then. Therefore, to be effective, improvement programs should try to close the gap between where one is now and where one wants to be now, not at some arbitrarily selected point in the future, and we should work backward from where we want to be to where we are in order to find a way of getting from where we are to where we want to be. Implementation of effective planning should consist of continuous efforts to close the gap between where we are and where we want to be at that time.

In creative improvement programs it is not necessary, as it is in TQM, to forecast the future; but it is necessary to take the future into account. Unfortunately, in an environment such as ours, in which change and complexity are increasing at an accelerating rate, our ability to forecast is deteriorating significantly. Fortunately, there is a way to do so without forecasting, by making assumptions about it. For example, it is not because we forecast that we are going to have a flat tire on our next automobile trip that we carry a spare tire in our car. In fact, if we were to forecast at all, it would be that we are *not* going to have a flat tire. But *we assume one is possible* and therefore prepare for this possibility. Preparation for possibilities constitutes *contingency planning*. Such planning requires only that we determine what futures are possible, not which one or ones are likely. Then we have a plan for as many of the possibilities as we can.

Corporations cannot forecast accurately what future inflation, interest, and exchange rates will be, not to mention competitive and governmental behavior. But they can specify the range of possibilities and develop a contingency plan for each.

However, there is in principle an even better way of dealing with the future, one that is often possible in practice. We do not forecast the weather in the buildings in which we work—nor do we need to—because buildings are artifacts created to enable us to *control* the weather. *Control of a variable eliminates the need to forecast and prepare for what is forecast.* Where it is not possible or feasible, contingency planning is the best alternative. Management should be building buildings where it can; where it can't, it should engage in contingency planning, not in predicting the future and preparing for that predicted future.

Summarizing, we can effectively deal with the future by either increasing our control of it or by making assumptions about the rest, preparing contingency plans based on these assumptions. Either of these procedures provides us with greater assurance that we will be where we want to be in the future than preparing for a predicted future.

Feasibility. When we stand where we want to be and look back at where we are, we see that we can get much closer to where we want to be than when we look forward from where we are to where we want to be. The reason for this is that most of the obstructions between us and where we want to be are in our minds, not "out there," in others or the environment. When we look to where we want to be from where we are, we tend to project self-imposed constraints on external sources that are out of our control. For example, we tend to decide what others will or will not do, and what they will or will not permit us to do. These decisions are frequently wrong and, however unintentionally, operate as self-fulfilling prophesies. Consider the following example.

The Clark Michigan Company, a wholly owned subsidiary of the Clark Equipment Company, was on the verge of bankruptcy in the early 1980s when James Rinehart took over as CEO of the parent company. Because Clark Michigan had negative cash flow, its future was limited to only about eighteen months. Its creditors threatened to put it into bankruptcy by then if it did not "turn itself around." To a large extent it was in this mess because a new competitor from Japan, Komatsu, had brought into the marketplace better equipment than Clark's at a price that was lower than it cost Clark to make its inferior equipment. Studies done by Clark showed that there was not enough time or money available to redesign either the product line or its production process so as to be competitive. Therefore it had adopted the strategy of dressing itself up for sale. Then Rinehart was appointed CEO.

Rinehart put Clark Michigan's managers through an idealized design exercise in which they had to design an immediate replacement of their company. Although they were reluctant to engage in what seemed to them to be such a fruitless exercise, they were very excited by the design they produced because they believed that, if it came into existence, it would be able to compete very effectively against Komatsu and others in the industry. However, they were frustrated by their belief that there was no way for the company to get from where it was to where they wanted it to be ideally.

Rinehart put them back to work, this time working backward. He asked them to see what combination of existing companies would give them the closest possible approximation to their idealized design. Much to their surprise, the managers found that a combination of four companies—one German, one Swedish, one Japanese, and their own—would yield such an approximation. But again they did not see the feasibility of getting these company together into a joint effort. Clark certainly did not have the resources to acquire other companies even if they were available. And why would another company want to join one that was on the verge of bankruptcy?

Nevertheless, Rinehart insisted on showing their design to the companies involved and discussing some kind of collaboration with them. The management of Mercedes-Benz, which owned the Euclid Truck Company, responded by offering that company to Clark for purchase. Clark explained it was not in a financial position to purchase it. However, they worked out an exchange of Euclid for stock in Clark.

The executives of AB Volvo were equally excited by the design, but they expressed doubt that German, Swedish, and American managers could work together effectively. They were concerned about what they called "cultural differences." At Rinehart's suggestion a team of managers from Volvo, Clark Michigan, and Euclid was set up in April 1985 to design a joint venture that approximated the last design as closely as possible. Again he had them working backward from where they wanted to be. That design was completed in September without any cultural problems arising within the team, and it was presented with unanimous team support to Volvo's and Clark's boards. It was approved by these boards, and in April 1986 the VME (Volvo, Michigan, Euclid) corporation was created. It is now one of the largest companies in its industry *and it is profitable.* Remember, Clark's managers had been able to "find no way out" when they worked from where the company was to where they wanted it to be. Working backward from where wants to be reveals a great deal more progress toward where one wants to be than when working forward from where one is.

Process and Theory

TQM has its origin in statistical quality control, which provided an effective way of reducing defects in products or services. Over time, additional procedures and practices were developed that contributed to the effectiveness of quality control; for example, quality circles and consensus decision-making. TQM's development has to a large extent been based on experience; little theory has been involved. As a result, its various components do not hang together as a cohesive whole. It tends to be an aggregate (a euphemism for a hodgepodge) of procedures and practices rather than a systemic process.

More importantly, TQM raises some issues it is not equipped to handle. For example, it tries to change management's activity from supervision, control of the actions of subordinates, to leadership, guiding their interactions and encouraging and facilitating their development. But it provides no theory to guide managers in efforts to create organizational structures that facilitate the management of interactions and the development of subordinates. Interactive and developmental management—that is, leadership—is seriously obstructed in conventional hierarchies to which TQM does not provide an alternative. On the other hand, the circular organization, described in detail in Chapter 4, is just such an alternative.

TQM implicitly assumes that the organization in which it is installed and applied has a relatively stable structure. The fact is that the time between reorganizations of most enterprises in the United States is less than the time required to install, let alone apply, TQM. Therefore, organizational re-structuring is frequently an obstruction to the application of TQM. Can organizations be designed so that restructuring is not frequently required? The answer is "yes." The multidimensional organization, described in Chapter 6, eliminates the need for periodic reorganization.

Nor does TQM deal with measures of performance and compensation systems that act as incentives for the type of behavior it seeks to encourage. These have a very significant effect on organizational behavior and on the behavior of individuals within organizations. Therefore, if these measures are left unchanged, whatever else is done, behavior will not change significantly, and those changes that are made will not last long. (For the types of measures and compensation required, see Gharajedaghi and Geranmayeh, chapter 12 in Choukroun and Snow, 1992.)

The most serious and common error that arises in the use of TQM is the failure to distinguish between *efficiency* and *effectiveness*. Efficiency has to do with the probability that a means will produce a specified outcome and the amount of resources it consumes in doing so. The greater this probability and the less the resources consumed, the more efficient is the means. Effectiveness is the product of efficiency and *the value of the outcome*. TQM can just as easily be applied to the production of poison gas as to a life-saving pharmaceutical. In itself, this is not a defect, but the failure to consider whether poison gas is an appropriate product *is* a serious defect. For example, TQM has been used extensively by the Japanese to improve the quality of their automobiles. But it has not raised questions about the rationality or appropriateness of the automobile as it is presently conceived. It has become increasingly apparent that automobiles are creating monumental problems such as air pollution, excessive dependence on fossil fuels, congestion, and a great deal of slaughter and disabling. Automobiles that can avoid these problems have been designed, but they require fundamental rather than incremental changes. It takes a lot more leadership and courage to induce and lead fundamental change than incremental improvements. As Peter Drucker is reported to have said, doing things right is very different from doing the right things. It has also been said that doing the right thing poorly is much better than doing the wrong thing perfectly.

Ethical evaluation of the product or service whose quality is to be improved should be but seldom is a part of any quality improvement program.

Conclusion

Enterprises conceptualized as social systems are seen to have two principal societal functions: to produce and to distribute wealth, wealth being the difference between the consumption they make possible and what they consume. To the extent that they fulfill these functions, they contribute to the standard of living of all their stakeholders. The appropriate objective of the enterprise itself when conceived as a social system is development, increasing ability and desire to satisfy its own needs and legitimate desires and those of others. The others whose needs and desires are most affected by what the enterprise does are the employees first; the consumers second; and third, those in the societies occupied by the enterprise who are affected by it. The best index of development is quality of life. Therefore, to the extent that the enterprise contributes to the development of its employees, it improves their quality of work life. To the extent that their quality of work life improves, the quality they put into the products and services they provide also goes up, and this improves the quality of lives of those who consume them. The currently growing concern with quality of life and quality of products and services reflects the growing tendency of people to conceptualize enterprises, institutions, organizations, governments, or even societies as social systems. These are systems that have purposes of their own; some of their parts have purposes of their own; and they are parts of larger systems that have purposes of their own. These containing systems contain other social systems, which in turn have purposes of their own.

I have argued that quality of life is largely a matter of aesthetics; that it involves satisfactions to be derived from anything we do, no matter how trivial. These are satisfactions derived from the intrinsic values, the satisfaction immediately experienced, and from the extrinsic values that arise out of a sense of progress toward ideals. Measurement of these two types of value may be possible in principle but currently not in practice. However, such measures are necessary only for those who are trying to improve the quality of life of others, not for those who attempt to improve their own quality of life, particularly if they are trying to do so while engaged in organizational planning. Involvement in a future-creating process can itself be a source of aesthetic satisfaction, fun, hence an improvement in the participants' quality of life. Moreover, its outcome can yield further improvements in this quality. The key to improved quality of life is not planning for others but planning for oneself. One cannot develop others, but by engaging them in planning, one can encourage and facilitate their development.

Efforts to improve the quality of work life and the quality of the products of work that are designed by those who must implement them generally do better than programs designed by others and imposed on them. Their commitment to programs that they helped design is much greater than to those designed by others. Experts can help the workforce in its design effort, but they should not replace it; they should be used only as the workforce sees fit.

Quality of work life (an input) and quality of products or services (work's output) interact strongly. Where quality of work life is poor, no effort to improve quality of outputs will yield lasting results. Disgruntled employees are not about to provide quality products or services. Their deliberate withholding of quality is a way of "getting even" with employers who do not provide the kind of work and work life they want.

On the other hand, if a high quality of work life is provided, quality of products and services usually comes without any special effort. People who enjoy what they are doing normally try to do it as well as they can, and take responsibility for the quality of their output. They take pride in what they do and seek the approval and appreciation of those who are affected by it.

Unless quality of work life is put right, total-quality-management (TQM) programs are bound to yield disappointing results. (This opinion is strongly reinforced by Rosenbluth, 1992.)

How can an organization be designed to provide the participative decision-making required for a high quality of work life while simultaneously enabling its management to deal effectively with the interactions of the parts managed, and of the whole they manage with other parts of the organization and its environment? This is the subject of the next chapter.

Chapter 4

The Circular Organization

This chapter is devoted to two very important and fundamental issues raised in earlier chapters. The first concerns improvement of the quality of work life of an increasingly educated work force and by so doing to serve better both their purposes and those of the organization as a whole. The second concerns the types of organizational changes required to facilitate the management of the way the parts of an organization interact, and the way the organization as a whole interacts with parts of its environment. In this chapter I present an organizational design that addresses these two issues. First, however, I review and amplify the issues.

Quality of Work Life

As the educational level and the amount of publicly and privately provided economic security of nonmanagerial employees in organizations have increased, the more they expect a satisfying quality of working life. The quantity and quality of their

outputs tend to be highly correlated with the amount of satisfaction they derive from their work. For this reason, the quality
of working life has been receiving increasing attention. Job
rotation, work enrichment, personal development programs,
and semiautonomous work groups are among the many inno-
vations directed at improving this quality. However, early on it
became apparent that unless *participation* in relevant decision-
making is increased, other changes produce only temporary
improvements in employee and organizational performance.

To increase employee participation, *communication* was
first improved: The flow of information down, up, and across
organizations was increased. This gave employees a better
grasp of what was going on, but not necessarily why. Improved
communication did not empower employees in any way; it did
not enable them to do anything they had not been able to do
before, but it did enable them to do some of those things
better. As a result, only marginal improvements in performance were obtained.

To obtain greater improvements, *consultation* was added to
communication; superiors solicited opinions and advice from
their subordinates. The opinions and advice received might or
might not be heeded by those who received them. Therefore,
although consultation gave employees opportunities to *influence* decisions that affected them, it gave them no *control* over
these decisions. Since many of the decisions with which they
were confronted were ones they believed they could make better than the managers who consulted them, the failure to heed
their advice often led to deterioration of their morale and performance.

Finally, it was recognized that without *codetermination*—
participation (a vote) in making relevant decisions—a full
commitment to work and the employer was not obtainable. At
every level of an organization, the quality of a person's work life
is proportional to that person's participation in decisions by
which he or she is affected. In turn, the need for such partici-

pation is proportional to the educational level of the worker: The more educated, the greater the need to participate. However, this need is matched by a corresponding need of managers to get their decisions and those made at higher levels implemented by educated workers. The more educated workers are, the easier it is for them to sabotage their managers' decisions. Managers cannot effectively implement their decisions in the current work environment unless they understand that there are two very different kinds of power—*power over* and *power to*—and how these relate to their ability to implement successfully.

Power over is the ability to get people to do things that they do not want to do, that they would not do voluntarily. This type of power is normally based on the ability to reward and punish. Autocratic rulers, dictators, military commanders, and parents of the very young have such power. On the other hand, power to is the ability to get people to do voluntarily what one wants them to. To exercise this ability is to *lead* rather than to command.

Under certain conditions, power over and power to may be opposed to each other. For example, shortly before the fundamentalists' revolution in Iran, I was asked by the empress, the shahbanoo, why her husband, the shah, who was one of most powerful rulers on Earth, could not successfully implement most of the programs he introduced. Here was a ruler who had almost complete power over his nationals, but virtually no power to implement his decisions. His impotence was explained by the fact that he had significantly increased the educational level of the Iranian population. Educated people do not respond well to commands, the exercise of power over.

The more educated a population or workforce, the more negatively correlated are power over and power to. This is particularly apparent in the case of very-high-tech industries, think tanks, and universities. Their chief executives cannot obtain what they want by ordering it. They have very little ability to enforce any decisions that are important to their professional staff and are not supported by it. Management can tell the professional staff what it would like to obtain but not how to pursue it. The principal task of such managers is to motivate, if not inspire, the staff and to create an environment in which, largely through self-determination, it serves the purposes of the organization as a whole. No wonder running such an organization has been compared to trying to herd a bunch of cats.

Resistance to change within organizations is commonplace. The effectiveness of such resistance increases with the educational level of those resisting. Decisions that involve significant organizational changes are often diluted or subverted during their implementation because those who must do the implementing do not "buy into" them. No matter how much authority decision-makers in large organizations have, they seldom can control or even monitor every step in the implementation of their decisions. Therefore, the more complex the organization managed, the more difficult it is for managers to exercise hands-on control of implementation of their decisions. Managers must increasingly depend on the willingness of their subordinates to act voluntarily in the way their managers want them to act. The readiness, willingness, and ability of an organization to change increases with the support of *all* of its members who would be affected by the change, not just those at the top.

Furthermore, recall that today most subordinates know how to do their jobs better than their bosses do. In the past, managers usually came up from the ranks; they were selected from among those to be managed and usually because they were better at what they did than any of their peers. When this was the common practice, most managers could do the job of their subordinates better than they could. Today, however, many managers never did the kind of work their subordinates do. They moved into their employing corporations from a university or from a managerial job in another corporation. In either case, they did not enter corporations at the bottom and work their way up. Moreover, in some organizations potential managers are systematically rotated among parts of a corporation in order to develop a view of the whole and to gain understanding of how the parts interact. (This, of course, is very much to be desired of those who are to become general managers.) However, as a result of higher-level entry and rotation of managerial personnel, today many if not most subordinates can do their jobs better than their bosses. Those subordinates who can't do their jobs at least as well as their bosses are generally replaced.

Therefore, today most bosses can tell their subordinates what output they want, but not how to get it. The ability to use all of one's relevant knowledge at work—to do as well as one knows how—contributes to one's quality of working life, and the quality of one's working life affects how much of one's relevant knowledge one wants to use at work. Therefore, managers should create environments in which their subordinates can and want to do as well as they know how.

When people are given the opportunity to participate in decisions that are among the most onerous to them, contrary to what one might expect, they tend to participate constructively and without ill will. For example, Frank Zaffino, a vice president of Kodak who headed the Kodak Apparatus Division, was instructed by the corporate executive office to reduce his division's management by a large percentage. Rather than proceed as most managers would, he called together all his managers and revealed the directive he had received. He then asked the assembled managers to come up with a policy and criteria that would guide him in deciding who should go. The group met several times and generated what he asked for. He then applied the policy and criteria they provided and opened his decisions to their inspection. Only one of the many managers affected raised a question about the fairness of the process, and he did not press his objection.

The quality of working life of an educated workforce depends on the extent to which its members can be self-controlling and participate in making those decisions that affect them directly. In other words, their quality of working life depends on how democratically their workplaces are organized. But herein lies the rub!

Work is organized only when it has to be divided. Divided labor must be coordinated. When there is a large number of coordinators, they, too, must be coordinated, and so on. This gives rise to hierarchy, and hierarchy is essential in organizations; it is the framework, the skeleton, around which organizations are built. And hierarchies are assumed to be necessarily autocratic.

This assumption is used to explain why most of the organizations and institutions, even government agencies, in a democratic society are managed autocratically. It is argued that they need hierarchy to organize work, and that hierarchy is necessarily autocratic. Those who are bothered by the irony of this try to soften hierarchical autocracy by decentralizing some of the decision-making.

Decentralization gives lower-level personnel the right to make decisions normally made at a higher level. However, although it can "soften" autocracy, it does not reduce it as long as the decision of any manager other than the one at the top can be overridden by one at a higher level. Where this is the case, those who make decentralized decisions generally try to make the decision they think their superiors would make if they were making it. Decentralization increases democracy only if the autonomy of lower-level organizational units is increased. Their autonomy is increased when it is realized that units at every level of an organization are best equipped to make some decisions without fear of being overridden.

All this gives rise to these questions: *Is a democratic hierarchy possible?* And if it is, *What would it look like?* These are questions that this chapter attempts to answer.

The Management of Interactions

In Chapter 1 I pointed out that the performance of systems, including corporations, is not the sum of the performances of its parts taken separately, but the product of their interactions. Organizational performance depends on both the interactions of its parts, and its interactions with other systems in its environment. Awareness of this raises to consciousness the need for managers to focus on interactions rather than actions. However, most corporations and other types of social systems are organized to facilitate the management of actions, telling others not only what to do but also how to do it, not interactions. In fact, in many organizations, interacting across at least some unit boundaries is either prohibited or discouraged.

Corporate personnel are usually identified by the function or business unit with which they are associated, and they are often discouraged from going around their managers to communicate or interact with personnel in other functions or business units. "Go through channels" is one of the most common "rules of the game," and this is a very effective way of suppressing interactions.

Within-organization interactions are of two types: horizontal and vertical. Horizontal interactions involve others at the same level of the organization. Management of this type of interaction is what we mean by coordination. Vertical interactions involve interacting with others who are at different levels of the organization. Management of this type of interaction constitutes integration.

In addition, managers have to be concerned with interactions with external organizations with which the unit managed is interdependent. These may be suppliers, wholesalers, retailers, independent sales agents, and so on. The increasing attention given recently to forming strategic alliances derives from recognition of the need to have better-integrated and better-coordinated interactions with related external enterprises. Whether interdependent enterprises are part of the same containing organization is not nearly as important as whether their interactions are well managed. There is no evidence that common ownership reduces conflict among interdependent activities. Peter Drucker is reported to have observed that there is more competition within corporations than among them, and that it is a lot less ethical.

Currently there is no systemic way of managing interactions with either internal or external organizations. Ad hoc arrangements seem to be the order of the day. Are there formal organizational arrangements that can assure the effective management of internal and external interactions? The answers to this and the preceding question—Is a democratic hierarchy possible?—lie in a type of organization called circular.

The Circular Organization

A description of the circular organization was first published by Ackoff (1981). At that time it had been applied to only a few organizations. Since then it has been used in a number of corporations and about a dozen government agencies in the United States and abroad. The design was, and continues to be, presented as a theme on which each organization that uses it is expected to compose its own variation. Each variation should take into account the unique characteristics of the organization involved. As a result, no two applications have been exactly the same.

A circular organization is a democratic hierarchy. A democracy has three essential characteristics: (1) the absence of an ultimate authority, the circularity of power; (2) the ability of each member to participate directly or though representation in all decisions that affect him or her directly; and (3) the ability of members, individually or collectively, to make and implement decisions that affect no one other than the decision-maker or decision-makers. In a hierarchy, each person other than the highest authority is subject to a higher authority. In a democracy, anyone who has authority over others is subject to the collective authority of these others; hence its circularity.

The main structural characteristic of a circular organization is that every person in a position of authority—every executive, manager, and supervisor—is provided with a board. First consider the composition of these boards, then their functions (responsibilities), and finally how they operate (Fig. 4.1).

As we proceed, keep in mind that the design is a theme around which each organization should compose its own variation. Except for the opportunity of nonmanagerial subordinates to participate voluntarily on their manager's board, no aspect of the design is "cast in concrete."

Composition of the Boards

Each board, except the ones at the top and bottom of the organization, ideally should have the following *minimal* membership: the manager whose board it is, that manager's immediate subordinates, and that manager's immediate superior. Therefore, in the board of a manager who has more than two subordinates, the subordinates constitute a majority if no others are added.

Any board has the right to add members drawn from inside or outside the organization. For example, boards of functionally defined corporate units such as marketing or finance commonly invite managers of other functional units to participate. Boards of units that have other internal units that consume their products or services—for example, accounting and R&D units—frequently invite some of the heads of their consuming units to join them. External customers and consumers have also been invited to join boards. In geographically dispersed organizations, such as multinational corporations, area-defined units have invited representatives of the nations and

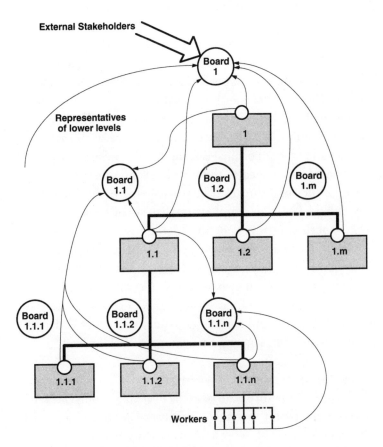

Fig. 4.1. A circular organization.

communities in which they operate to participate on their boards. These have included representatives of relevant consumer or environmental groups.

The principle involved in adding members to most boards is that in so doing they improve representation of their principal stakeholders. Most units within an organization have internal stakeholders, and many have some that are external. If a unit of an organization has no internal stakeholders—that is, no other part of the organization is affected by what it does—

serious consideration should be given to this question: Why should it be part of the corporation?

In general, it is not desirable for a board to permit the number of representatives of any one type of stakeholder to exceed the number of subordinates on it. The subordinates need not constitute a majority. (As will be seen, since decisions are not made by majority rule, this does not significantly reduce their authority.) However, the most effective boards are ones in which the subordinates form the largest subgroup and, if any people are added to the board beyond those minimally required, the subordinates have participated in deciding who they should be. This emphasizes that subordinates are the most important members of any board.

Additions to a board may be either ad hoc, temporary, or permanent. They may be voting members, have restricted voting privileges (where they have a special competence or interest), or be advisory with no voting rights. Those who are less than full-voting members may also be asked to attend only designated meetings in which their particular knowledge or position is relevant.

High-level management boards in corporations have commonly created advisory boards, each consisting of only one type of stakeholder—for example, Anheuser-Busch has a board consisting of elected representatives of its wholesalers, National Life of Vermont has one of its agents, and a number of corporations have technical advisory boards. Such boards normally address only questions or issues put before them by the management board to which they are appended.

In a unionized organization, union officials are usually invited to participate on boards established at their levels of responsibility—shop stewards at lower levels, department representatives at a higher level, and union executives at the highest level. The union or local that participates on boards of a circularly organized corporation should be encouraged to organize its headquarters in the same way.

The board at the top. Corporations already have boards of which their CEOs, and frequently some of their subordinates, are members. An ideal corporate board should contain representatives of all its stakeholders, including employees at all levels. However, CEOs should also have management boards that differ from corporate boards. These management boards should consist of all managers who report directly to the CEOs, and if they do not chair the corporate board, their chairpersons. Where the CEOs are chairpersons, one or more members of the executive committee of their corporate boards should be on their management boards.

Where an executive or manager has a staff, as many do, a separate staff board is usually established. If that staff has a head other than the manager whose staff it is, then it will be that chief of staff's board, but with the executive or manager to whom the manager reports participating. If the executive or manager doubles as chief of staff, the manager's immediate superior is generally not included on the staff board.

The boards at the lowest level. The boards of managers and supervisors at the lowest level of the organization should include all their subordinates. If they have more than about ten subordinates, their boards are likely to be unwieldy. However, we have learned from experience not to reduce the number on a board by having subordinates elect representative to serve on their manager's board. *All employees should have an opportunity to serve on their immediate superiors' boards.*

Boards have not operated successfully where representatives of workers rather than all the workers have been used. The reason is not obscure. On the one hand, the representatives are usually treated by the managers on the board like workers rather than colleagues, particularly if they are unionized. The lowest-level managers and supervisors in most organizations have the greatest difficulty in ignoring the status line that separates them from their subordinates; rank is terribly important to them. On the other hand, the representatives of the workers serving on the board begin to understand some of management's decisions that would previously have seemed irrational to them, and they try to defend these decisions before the workers. This makes the workers view them as representatives of management. As a result, the representatives feel that they occupy a no-man's-land between the workers and their manager or supervisor. They do not stay on the boards for long. This is why all employees should be able to participate on their immediate superiors' boards.

Where the number of subordinates is too large to have all of them serve on one board, they should be divided into semiautonomous work groups. Each group should then select a leader who reports to the lowest-level manager. But the group leader selected by the workers is given a board that consists of the group leader, the manager to whom the leader reports, and all other members of the group. Unlike the use of representatives, this arrangement has never run into difficulty. Furthermore, this arrangement makes it possible to reduce the number of lowest-level managers. For example, assume that eight is a good average span of control. Then eight groups of eight each, or sixty-four, can report to the lowest-level managers. This is very likely to be more than reported to them before the formation of the semiautonomous work groups. This reduces the number of lowest-level managers required.

The lowest-level work groups should decide for themselves how to select their leaders and for how long they should serve.

Where higher-level managers have more subordinates than make for effective boards, similar formation of semiautonomous work groups should take place. In general, however, the spans of control of managers in the United States are too small rather than too large. My experience indicates an average of slightly more than three. (In Japan the average is almost three times as large.) Where managers have fewer than five subordinates, their responsibilities should be reconsidered and, where possible, extended. The larger the average span of control of managers, the fewer levels of management are required. The fewer levels of management there are in an organization, the more interaction can take place among different levels. With an average span of control of eight, an organization of five levels can have almost 33,000 members, and of six levels can have approximately 262,000 members!

The span that a manager can control depends on how dissimilar are the functions of those controlled and the amount of interaction between or among them. If they all have exactly the same functions and are relatively independent of each other—for example, managers of identical McDonald's restaurants—the span can be quite large. On the other hand, if their functions are very different and they interact intensely, few managers can effectively coordinate ten or more. Miller (1956) has shown that seven is the number of distinct activities that a manager can think about simultaneously, hence interdependently. Nine is the number for exceptional people and five for less-than-average people.

Participation on boards is generally made compulsory for managers but voluntary for others. Voluntary participation on boards by those who do not have to participate provides a very good indication of their value to them. There is obviously something wrong with boards that fail to attract a majority of their manager's nonmanagerial subordinates. The reasons for such a failure should be determined by the relevant manager's immediate superior, and corrective action should be taken. Where this has occurred, the most common reason has been that the subordinates believe their bosses will not manage the boards democratically, or they have already not done so. Since they are more often right than wrong, a serious reevaluation of the manager involved is indicated. Again, managers of educated subordinates cannot be effective if not supported by their subordinates.

It should be noted that in a circular organization managers

other than those at the two top and two bottom levels of the hierarchy will interact directly with *five* levels of management. They interact with two higher levels and their own level on their superiors' boards, and with two lower levels on their subordinates' boards. Managers at the second level from the top and bottom interact with managers at four levels, and those at the bottom with three. Those at the top have representatives of multiple levels of management on their boards. Therefore, boards makes it possible to manage both vertical and horizontal interactions and therefore to achieve higher degrees of coordination and integration of activities, policies, and plans, than conventionally organized and managed enterprises attain.

Responsibilities of the Boards

Fully empowered boards have six responsibilities:

1. planning for the unit whose board it is;
2. policymaking for the unit whose board it is;
3. coordinating plans and policies of the immediately lower level;
4. integrating plans and policies—its own and those of its immediately lower level—with those made at higher levels;
5. improving the quality of work life of the subordinates on the board;
6. enhancing and evaluating the performance of the manager whose board it is.

Planning. Each board has responsibility for planning for the unit whose board it is and for continuously monitoring the implementation and effects of its plans. It should redirect the plan whenever it goes off track; even the best of plans tends to do this. It is the responsibility of the board to see to it that the plans it prepares have a beneficial effect on the unit planned for. (For a discussion of the different types of planning available and their relative advantages and disadvantages, see Ackoff, 1981.)

Upper-level managers frequently have a planning staff, but this staff should *not* prepare plans for the board. Through supporting activities it should enable the board to prepare better plans than it would have otherwise. Planning can be like a ritual rain dance performed at the end of the dry season: It can have no effect of the weather that follows, but it can make those who engage in it feel good and mistakenly think they are in control. The principal benefit to be derived from planning may not come from implementing the plans produced but from producing them. In planning, process is often the most important product. The reason is that by engaging in it one can come to understand how the parts interact to affect the performance of the whole. This enables the parts of an organization to focus on the performance of the whole rather than on their own. Recall that when every part of an organization taken separately performs as well as possible, the whole does not.

Policy. Boards also have responsibility for making and monitoring policies applicable to their units and their subsidiaries. Implementation of policies is the responsibility of appropriate managers. A policy is a decision *rule*, not a decision. Regulations and laws are decision rules. For example, "hire only college graduates for managerial positions" is a policy; hiring such a person is a decision. Boards should not make decisions other than those directly affecting the quality of working life of their members. Except for these, managers make the decisions, not boards. Therefore, boards are not management committees; they are analogous to the legislative branch of government, and managers to the executive branch. The British Parliament does not implement or execute; it enacts and it monitors. The prime minister participates in legislation, but his or her primary responsibility is to execute the acts of Parliament and to recommend such acts to it. Boards and their managers are similarly related.

The use of boards in an advisory role is common, and also to facilitate communication up, down, and across. When managers consult their boards on decisions for which they are responsible, that responsibility remains with them; it is not transferable to their boards. When boards are used to advise and facilitate communication, the need for separate meetings of staffs, committees, task forces, counsels, and other types of groups is reduced if not eliminated, as I shall discuss later.

Boards are free to implement any plans or policies they make that do not affect another part or other parts of the organization, or for which they have sufficient resources. Where a plan or policy affects another part or other parts of the organization, either the approval of the affected part or parts must be obtained before it can be implemented, or, where agreement of the affected units cannot be obtained, approval of the lowest-level board at which all units affected converge. Where additional resources are required, a request for them must go to the lowest level of management that can provide the resources required. These requirements, together with the co-ordinating and integrating functions of boards, enable managers to control interactions of lower-level units. They also provide a great deal of autonomy to lower-level units because they can implement more than half the plans and policies they make without approval from above.

Such increased autonomy of subordinate units often causes concern for higher-level managers. For example, a vice president in charge of production in a large corporation called me one day and expressed great distress over what boards at the shop-floor level had collectively decided to do. They had decided to eliminate time cards and time clocks. They argued that no other units in the company would be affected. The vice president told me he was not sure that this was true. More important to him, however, was that there were sections of the plant that, if not manned, would shut down the rest of the plant. How, he asked, could he prevent this from occurring without controlling his workers' time at assigned stations? I asked him if he thought the workers were aware of the vulnerability of the plant to these critical sections. He said they were. Then I asked what he thought they expected him to do if the plant had to be shut down because one of these sections was unmanned. He said he believed that they would expect him to reinstate the time-controlled system they had replaced. Why, then, I asked, would they want to replace the old system unless they were sure they could avoid a plant shutdown, particularly since they would suffer financially from such a shutdown? He thought about this for a while and reluctantly decided to let the workers go ahead with their plan.

Several weeks later, he called to tell me that the quantity and quality of the plant's output had increased significantly. I asked him how the workers had managed this. He said he didn't know and he wasn't going to try to find out. He had learned an important lesson: *Let your subordinates do what they know how to do better than you do.*

Coordination and integration. To coordinate is to manage horizontal interactions; to integrate is to manage vertical interactions. Each board is responsible for seeing to it that the plans and policies made by its immediately subordinate boards are compatible—that is, for coordinating them. Since the managers at the level immediately below that of each board are members of that board, coordination is self-coordination with participation of two higher levels of management. If subordinate managers on any board want to coordinate their activities with peers who report to a manager other than theirs, they can either invite their peers to participate on their board, or hold joint meetings with their boards.

Each board is also responsible for seeing to it that the plans and policies prepared by its immediately subordinate boards are consistent with those made by it and higher-level boards—that is, for integrating the plans and policies made at different levels of the organization. Integration involves preservation of the hierarchy: No board should be permitted to make a plan or policy that is incompatible with a higher-level board's plan or policy. However, each board except the one at the top can easily request a revision of higher-level plans or policies because it contains members who participate on two higher-level boards. Moreover, because its members have an extended vertical view of the organization (covering as many as five levels), boards are not likely to make plans or policies that are harmful to lower level parts of the organization or incompatible with those made at higher levels.

Effective coordination and integration require understanding that consistency and compatibility are not the same thing. In many organizations there is the explicit or implicit requirement that the procedures and policies that apply in one unit should apply to all units at that or subordinate levels. For example, most corporations require that the same benefit package be available to workers in every part of the company. The demand for consistency among organizational units may actually reduce the effectiveness of some units. For example, a company with multiple locations that does not take local cost of living into account when setting salaries may be in for great difficulty in employing suitable people.

Quality of work life. Recall that quality-of-work-life decisions directly affect the satisfaction and sense of meaningfulness that employees at all levels of an organization derive from their work. As observed in Chapter 3, when employees are given the ability to affect their quality of work life, significant improvements in the quantity and quality of their work are usually attained. These improvements tend to be much more dramatic than those obtained by programs explicitly directed at increasing productivity and product or service quality.

The types of changes made by boards to improve their

members' quality of work life are frequently changes that managers would not think of. For example, in a manufacturing facility in the United States that employed mostly Mexican workers, management had recently installed a new and attractive cafeteria for the workforce. It offered good food at subsidized prices. However, most of the workers did not use the cafeteria; they preferred to use the food trucks that gathered outside the plant. When these workers were organized into boards, one of the first things they did was "Mexicanize" the menu of the cafeteria and install a Mexican cook. Utilization of the cafeteria soared.

In another manufacturing facility the workers arranged for a family day on which they could bring their families to the plants and show them how it operated and what they did. Management added a picnic on the plant grounds. It became a major annual event in the lives of all who worked at the plant, whatever their rank.

Enhancing and evaluating management. The most controversial responsibility that some boards have is for enhancing and evaluating the performance of the manager whose board it is. In a number of cases this function has been initially withheld from the boards. However, in most of these cases, it has been given to them subsequently.

Where boards have this responsibility, managers cannot retain or be appointed to their positions without approval of their boards, hence of their subordinates. This function eliminates an ultimate authority and therefore fulfills a requirement of democracy. In one large multinational company, managers cannot be appointed unless they have been interviewed and approved by those who will be their immediate subordinates, their peers who report to the same manager as the appointee will, and that superior. Managers appointed in this way seldom perform poorly. Just as subordinates can make their managers look bad, they can also make them look good.

Boards cannot fire their managers; they can only remove

them from their positions. Only a superior can fire a subordinate. This means that managers cannot hold their positions without the approval of *both* their bosses and their subordinates. It is hard to imagine how managers who do not have such approval can do their jobs adequately. Yet many managers lack such support, especially from their subordinates. Even superiors are hesitant to move a manager not supported by their subordinates if they are supported by a higher-level manager. The subordinate members of a board taken collectively tend to have more courage than they have taken separately. Therefore they are not likely to tolerate incompetence or obstructiveness from their immediate superior.

Nevertheless, there have been very few cases in which boards have removed their managers. They have not had to because they have been able to obtain most of what they want from their managers through constructive criticism, through exercise of their enhancement responsibility. This is usually accomplished in the following way. At least once each year the immediate subordinates of managers meet without their managers or their superiors to discuss what their bosses can do that would enable them to do their jobs more effectively. They do not discuss how their bosses might do their jobs more effectively. The subordinates are also precluded from telling their bosses what they should *not* do; they must confine themselves to suggesting what, in their opinion, their bosses *should* do. When they have organized and prioritized their suggestions, they meet with and present their suggestions to their manager.

In most cases, an experienced facilitator is used to lead the first such meeting of the subordinates. This facilitator is then often used to present the outputs of this meeting to the boss, but with the subordinates present. However, facilitators have very seldom been used in second and subsequent sessions.

The "receiving managers" are expected to respond to each suggestion in one of three ways. First, they can accept a suggestion. In my experience, they accept about 75 percent of the suggestions because they usually make sense but involve things the managers had not previously thought of. For example, one such group suggested that their boss use his full vacation allowance so they would not feel guilty if they used theirs. The boss was surprised to learn that his failure to use his vacation allowance was preventing his subordinates from using theirs. He accepted the suggestion and implemented it. Another board suggested more flexible budgets, particularly with respect to the purchase of minor equipment and external services. Again the boss agreed and appropriate changes were made. Still another board suggested that the actions of higher-level boards be reported to them immediately after these boards meet.

Second, receiving managers can reject a suggestion, but if they do so, they are obliged to explain their rejection fully. In most cases their rejections involve constraints imposed on them from above, constraints of which their subordinates were unaware. Their subordinates do not have to agree with the reasons for the rejection, but they should understand them. There have been very few cases where such explanations did not produce the required understanding.

Finally, receiving managers can ask for more time to consider a suggestion and commit to a time by which they will respond to it. In general, they should respond within a month.

These constructively oriented "improvement" sessions have generally brought boss and subordinates much closer and bound them into a more collaborative relationship. In some cases these sessions have terminated overt hostility. They reflect the fundamental change in the concept of management that is implicit in the circular organization: *A principal responsibility of managers is to create an environment and conditions under which their subordinates can do their jobs as effectively as their capabilities allow.* It is not to supervise them.

In one very large company a new business unit was created as a result of a cross-departmental study I facilitated. The new unit was created to exploit what had previously been a by-product of the company. The chief operating officer of the corporation appointed a director of the new unit. He did so without consulting any of those who had been involved in generating the recommendation that the unit be created, or any of those who had previously had experience with the product involved. Moreover, the person he appointed was much younger than many of those who were to report to him directly, and came from a staff, rather than a line, function. Resentment of this appointment among those who had to report to him ran very high.

The newly appointed director installed management boards throughout the organization, but they were received with suspicion. His own board never operated smoothly or with good will. When consulted about this by the manager in charge, I suggested a session of his subordinates directed at enhancing his performance. He agreed and asked me to facilitate it.

It was a very difficult meeting to facilitate because of pervasive ill will. The inclination of the participants was to "bitch" rather than make any constructive suggestions. Nevertheless, with considerable prodding they eventually produced a prioritized list of such suggestions and for each selected a member to present it to the director. A meeting with the director was then convened. He responded very positively to the first five or six suggestions, saying that had he been aware of the deficiencies involved he would have corrected them without prompting, but he expressed his appreciation for having them brought to his attention. At this point the oldest of his subordinates, the man who had expected to be appointed as director, diverted the meeting to say something he urgently wanted to say. He told the director that he had resented his appointment and consequently had done all he could to make the director look bad. He was now sorry he had acted in this way; he realized now that he had had no reason to take out his disappointment on the young head of the unit. He promised that his hostile behavior would stop and that he would be fully cooperative in the future.

The head of the unit then confessed that he had been aware of the older man's opposition and that he had made unsuccessful efforts to get him transferred to another unit. He then apologized for this effort and promised to be more supportive of his subordinates. The meeting then became a "born again" session in which everyone present got their former hostile feelings off their chests and promised cooperation in the future. That meeting created what has since been a very successful management team.

How Boards Operate

Boards should prepare their own operating procedures, but most of them operate in much the same way. Most, for example, operate by consensus rather than majority rule. The advantages of consensus over split decisions are apparent. The principal advantage is that it removes the possibility of a tyranny of the majority, the type of tyranny most frequently encountered. What is not apparent is how to obtain consensus when opinions differ significantly. Recall that in Chapter 3 I described ways by which it can be obtained when it does not come about spontaneously: by the use of tests or experiments to which all agree, or acceptance of the relevant manager's decision when complete agreement among his or her subordinates cannot otherwise be attained.

Most boards are chaired by the manager whose board it is. In a few cases they use a rotating chairmanship. In no case that I know of has a board selected as chairperson the superior of the manager whose board it is. This, it has been argued, would make a board too status-conscious and would discourage free expression of opinions.

Each board either designates one of its members as recording secretary, or uses a secretary who serves the manager whose board it is for this purpose. Minutes of each meeting are usually prepared and distributed shortly after each meeting. In most cases each meeting begins with a review of the status of tasks previously assigned and commitments previously made. The "secretary" of the board is responsible for maintaining this list and distributing it to all board members.

Agendas for meetings are usually prepared by the secretary of the board using inputs from any of the board members.

After the initial "break-in" period most boards schedule monthly meetings, which usually last two to three hours. When required, additional meetings are called either by the manager whose board it is or by any of its other members. Boards individually decide how often and when to meet. Some do it after work, some on weekends, some on lunch hours, and some even manage to hold them during working hours by rotating attendance.

Some Commonly Asked Questions

When first confronted with the concept of boards, many managers fear the worst. Here are some of the questions they ask, reflecting their fears.

Since managers may have ten or more boards to attend, when do they get their work done? When one chief executive who had installed boards throughout his company with considerable success was asked this question, he replied much as follows:

> The ten boards in which I take part meet once per month for three to four hours each. Say, four hours. That makes for about forty hours per month. If I worked only forty hours per week—I, like most managers, work closer to sixty—this would be only 25 percent of my time. According to a number of studies of how managers spend their time, most managers spend only about 20 percent of their time managing—that is, engaged in activities

that only a manager can carry out. Therefore, the question that should be asked is: What do I do with the other 55 percent of my time? The fact is that I now spend less time in meetings than I did previously because the boards have eliminated the need for most of them.

However, there is a better answer. In my boards I plan, make policy, coordinate the plans and policies at the level reporting to me, integrate these with those made at my level and the corporate board, and evaluate and guide the performance of my subordinates two levels down. What could I be doing that is more important than these things? Furthermore, the improved planning and policy-making have made my job easier and my decisions better.

Board meetings are normally held only if something is on the agenda; otherwise they are canceled. On the other hand, they are called together as soon as possible when a critical issue arises. The frequency of meetings obviously depends on the extent to which a board's members are geographically dispersed. In cases where they work in different countries, board meetings are held quarterly, for a full day or more, when the members of the board normally come together for other purposes as well. At the other end of the scale, where they all occupy the same office space, meetings can be called on very short notice. One such organization has installed a gong that any member of its board can strike, thereby calling a board meeting at once.

Does it take any special skills to run board meetings? Yes. It takes an ability to generate consensus, and this requires an ability to listen to and respect the opinions of others, even when they diverge from one's own. It also requires an ability to find what is common among a set of apparently divergent opinions. For this reason most organizations that initiate boards provide managers at all levels with training in group dynamics and consensus management. A large part of such training consists of enabling people to see themselves as others see them, and thereby better to understand the reactions their behavior evokes from others. Such training usually takes only two or three days. In many cases these sessions are made available to union and nonmanagerial personnel as well and are conducted with multiple levels attending.

Does it help to have a skilled facilitator at board meetings? It often does, especially in the first few meetings. A facilitator can help establish the rules of procedure and keep the meetings flowing smoothly and quickly. Once the manager whose board it is gains confidence in his or her ability to run these meetings, he or she should take over. Then it often helps for the facilitator to remain as an observer for at least the first few meetings run by the manager. This enables the facilitator to make constructive suggestions to the manager in charge.

An external facilitator can say things to senior managers that it would be very difficult for an insider to say. The following is a case in point.

In one company, a brilliant CEO whom I considered to be a close friend initiated his board with me as facilitator. He had such a high level of intelligence, so much more than his subordinates, that they were in awe of him. Consequently, when the first meeting of the CEO's board began, his subordinates would wait until they had heard his position on the issue raised before expressing their own opinion, which seldom diverged significantly from his. As a result, the meeting was only superficially participative. However, the CEO, who was anything but intentionally autocratic, was unaware of what was going on.

When it became clear to me that the board was not operating well, I pointed this out to the CEO and asked him to withhold his opinion until others had a chance to express theirs. He was embarrassed, apologized, and promised to hold his tongue. But when after the next issue was raised there was a silence while the subordinates were self-consciously deciding what to say, if anything, the CEO could not contain himself and broke out with his opinion. I asked him to leave the room.

He was surprised and asked me if I meant it seriously. I said I did, since the meeting was useless with him attending.

He left the room and about a half hour later opened the door, put his head in, and asked if he could return. I said he could if he sat in a corner and said nothing. Everyone laughed nervously, but he did as he was told. A while later, he asked if he could return to the table. I said he could if he withheld his views until others had spoken. He returned to the table and this time behaved as instructed. The board then operated properly and rapidly became a very good one. Among other things, it gave several of the CEO's subordinates an opportunity to "come out and show themselves," and they were worth seeing. He thought so and therefore came to feel that holding back his opinion had a significant payoff to him.

The number of boards set up at Metropolitan Life exceeded the number of external facilitators they could possibly get. Therefore, with the help of external facilitators, they set up a special training program to prepare internal facilitators. Most of those trained had previous experience running quality circles. Their transformation was relatively easy.

Have any of the organizations that started boards discontinued them? To the best of my knowledge only two organizations that installed boards subsequently discontinued their use. Both were military organizations, and both discontinued their boards for the same reason. Shortly after their initiation and before they were operating throughout the organizations, their commanding officers were replaced. The replacements discontinued the boards along with many other things initiated by their predecessors. Such discontinuations are common in the military; it is used as a way that new commanders can assert their individuality and authority.

What is the principal obstruction to the successful implementation of boards? Failure to obtain the commitment of middle managers. These managers seldom "buy in" unless they have (1) been exposed to the idea of boards before the decision is made to use them, (2) had an opportunity to discuss them with someone experienced in their use, and (3) had an opportunity to participate in the decision to use them. For this reason, it is essential that middle managers be "brought along" the way to implementation. Since there may be a large number of managers and they may be geographically dispersed, videotapes of relevant presentations and discussions have often been used to orient and inform managers. Availability of an experienced person to answer questions can help a great deal—a hot line.

What is usually done with managers who do not fully cooperate? As previously noted, participation in boards is usually required of managers; therefore evaluation of their participation on boards has been made a significant part of their performance reviews. Where boards have been introduced with a strong and unambiguous commitment of the chief executive officer, there have been very few managers who, after indoctrination, fail to participate fully. I have firsthand knowledge of only one case in which it was necessary to remove an uncooperative manager, but I have heard of a few others.

What is done with boards where such groups as quality circles already exist? In some cases they run in parallel, but in most cases the functions of the circles are incorporated into the boards, thereby reducing the number of meetings required. The composition of the boards is well suited to the needs of quality circles.

Where in an organization is the best place to initiate the use of boards? Wherever you are! Boards have been successfully initiated at every organizational level and have subsequently spread to other levels. At Anheuser-Busch, a board (called the"Policy Committee") was initially established at the top. After some of the executives involved had experience with it, they started boards of their own. Then boards moved down layer by layer. It took about a year for boards to reach the lowest levels in units whose chief executive encouraged their formation. In others they never did get all the way down.

At Kodak, the first boards (called "planning boards") were established in a unit whose manager was at the fifth level of the organization. Boards then spread up, down, and across. At Alcoa's Tennessee Operations, boards were simultaneously established at the top and bottom, with the participation of the union (Local 309 of the United Steel Workers) at both levels. Boards subsequently moved up and down the organization until they met at the middle, where resistance was greatest. In some organizations, such as Armco Latin America, most of the managers were indoctrinated at the same time; hence, boards were initiated all over the organization simultaneously in Argentina, Uruguay, Brazil, Chile, Peru, Ecuador, Venezuela, and Colombia. I have worked with boards in more than ten different countries and have never found culture to be an obstruction.

In some cases, as in the Ministry of Public Works in Mexico, a third-level manager initiated boards without the participation of his immediate superior, a deputy minister, who begged off, claiming to be too busy to be involved. The performance of this division became conspicuously outstanding. The deputy minister was the only one to be reappointed by the next president. He could find no reason for this other than his subordinate's success. Therefore, he reappointed his subordinate, joined his board, and required all other third-level managers who reported to him to initiate boards. Moreover, several newly appointed deputy ministers attributed the retention of the one holdover to his use of the boards, and they did likewise.

Senior executives are not always able to attend all the board meetings of their immediate subordinates because of other demands on their time. In such cases they are kept informed through minutes of meetings, and they are told when their attendance at an upcoming meeting is critical. They usually make such meetings.

Is it easier or more difficult to introduce boards in a unionized company? Both. Where unions have collaborated (as at

Alcoa's Tennessee Operations and at Super Fresh), they make it easier to involve the unionized workforce. Where they are opposed, it is difficult but possible to introduce boards. In a few such cases, unions have eventually come around to supporting the idea and to participating fully—for example, at Westinghouse Furniture Systems.

Are there certain types of organizational structures on which a circular organization cannot be superimposed—for example, a matrix organization? To the best of my knowledge, no. Since, in a matrix organization, almost everyone has two bosses, almost everyone participates on at least two boards. The circular organization design has been used by organizations with just about every type of structure. This should not be surprising because democracy is associated with a wide variety of governmental structures.

Conclusion

To introduce boards in an organization is not to put a bandage on it but to initiate a profound cultural change. The conversion of an autocratic state to one that is democratic has never been easy. (Witness what has happened and is happening to what was once the Soviet Union.) In a circular organization, managers are no longer commanders; they are not even supervisors. They are required to become leaders, facilitators, and educators. These are roles that many managers find difficult to assume. It takes time to convert them. However, the rewards for doing so can be very large. Recall the case of Alcoa's Tennessee Operations. These Operations were scheduled to be shut down because of their very low productivity and poor quality of product. In fewer than two years their productivity and product quality improved so much that Alcoa's executives reversed their decision. They subsequently initiated a very ambitious modernization program at Tennessee. At the end of 1987, the most advanced aluminum-sheet rolling mill in the world was opened at these Operations.

Recall also that earlier in this decade A&P closed all its supermarkets in the Delaware Valley, the metropolitan area of Philadelphia. Lack of profitability was the reason. Subsequently, in a joint effort with locals of the United Food & Commercial Workers, a new chain of supermarkets was participatively designed. The markets involved the use of boards at all levels. The new chain, called *Super Fresh*, was initiated mostly in the old facilities. It became the fastest-growing and most profitable chain in the area. It has since been successfully extended to other parts of the country.

Armco's Latin American Division (ALAD) was reorganized around the use of boards and, as a result, experienced significant improvements in performance as well as morale. The same has been true of a number of other organizations, including Tremec in Mexico, Metropolitan Life, Central Life Assurance, several new business units of Alcoa, and parts of Imperial Oil in Canada, Ford, and a variety of departments and divisions of Kodak.

Democracy and efficiency are not inimitable; in fact, they become more and more closely connected as the educational level and economic security of the workforce (or the citizens of a country) increase.

Such participation in decision-making as the circular organization makes possible can contribute significantly to the quality of work life. How much it contributes depends on how much autonomy is given to the organizational units involved, how much self-control they can exercise. But how does one get cooperative interaction among relatively autonomous organizational units that frequently have to compete for scarce corporate resources? This very important question is addressed in the next chapter.

Chapter 5

The Organization as a
Market Economy

The Problems Created by Nonmarket Economies

Today, a number of countries are trying to convert from a centrally planned and centrally controlled economy to a market economy. Not one national economy that is centrally planned and controlled has ever attained as high a level of economic development as has been attained by national market economies. Of course, not every national market economy has flourished, but every national economy that has flourished has been a market economy. Therefore, for nations, a market economy appears to be necessary though not sufficient to attain a high level of economic development.

Although the United States and most countries in Western Europe have market economies, most organizations, institutions, and government agencies in these countries do not. Their internal economies are more like the national economy that Russia is trying to get rid of than the national economies their countries have.

Many Western corporations are in decline partly because they either are monopolies, or they contain many units that are. The economies of monopolies are generally centrally planned and centrally controlled. In their search for economies of scale, centrally planned and centrally controlled economies in nations and corporations tend to create internal monopolistic providers of goods and services. For example, in most Western corporations such functionally defined departments as accounting, personnel, finance, and R&D are usually organized as subsidized monopolies. They are subsidized in the sense that they are budgeted from above; therefore, the users of their products or services do not pay for them directly. They are monopolies in the sense that their internal users are allowed no alternative source of supply. The funds used to support the subsidized units are obtained by taxing lower-level units, usually in a way that does not reflect the extent to which they use the internal monopolistic suppliers of goods and services. Such suppliers are generally insensitive and unresponsive to the users of their services, but they are sensitive and responsive to the sources of their subsidies. Their sources of financial support are usually more removed from the units served and less familiar with their needs and expectations than the serving units.

Monopolies tend to bureaucratize. Bureaucracies "make work"—that is, keep people busy doing nothing productive—but what they frequently do is create obstructions for those who have productive work to do. The ability of bureaucracies to survive is generally proportional to their size; hence growth is one of their major objectives. Bureaucratic monopolies are the principal sources of such dysfunctional properties as are now commonplace in corporations: oversizing, excessive layers of management, and spans of control that are too small. The current rash of downsizing—often euphemistically called "rightsizing"—is most often a symptom of previously uncon-strained and unjustified growth of internal bureaucratic mo-nopolies.

Even if unintentionally, centralized economic planning and control encourage subordinate organizational units to be-come bloated largely because those in control estimate the value of a unit by its size and compensate its manager accord-ingly.

In addition, because salaries are usually proportional to rank in American organizations, people are often promoted to managerial ranks not because managers are needed or they have managerial skills, but because this is the only way to obtain additional compensation for them. To justify the pro-motion, one or two people are assigned to them. This makes for very small spans of control which, in turn, leads to exces-sive layering. In one major company in the United States, I found that 20 percent of the managers had only one person reporting to them.

Centrally planned and centrally controlled economies also stimulate excessive increases of costs of internally provided products and services because the monopolistic supplying units do not need to compare their costs and prices with those of competing suppliers of the same products and services. As a result, neither the supplying units nor their subsidizers know what the costs of the units actually are. It is almost impossible to determine the economic value of a subsidized internal sup-plier who does not have to compete for customers. In a market economy, users, not subsidizers, evaluate suppliers and ex-press their evaluation in a way that counts, by their purchases.

Transfer pricing, which is the surrogate for market pricing in a centrally planned and centrally controlled economy, pro-duces intense internal conflict and competition. It is doubtful that transfer pricing can ever be acceptable, let alone fair, to both units involved. For example, a large producer of electrical and electronic goods had one division that was a very successful producer of small electric motors, and another that supplied replacement parts and components to distributors of electrical equipment. An executive vice president to whom both divisions reported required the manufacturing unit to provide the distributor-supplying unit with motors and the latter to use only motors supplied by the former. The same vice president established the transfer prices that were used. Both divisions were set up as business units,with profit maximization as one of their major objectives. Their executives were compensated as a function of their profitability. These conditions put the two divisions at war. The producing division was often called on to supply to the supplying division motors it could sell on the open market at higher than the transfer price. The supplying division often had to buy motors from the producing division at a higher transfer price than it could buy them for from external suppliers. Such conflict is commonplace where transfer pricing is involved.

Corporate units generally have more cooperative relationships with their external suppliers than with their internal suppliers. But even more serious is the fact that transfer pricing can contribute to the demise of an enterprise taken as a whole. Consider the account of the deterioration of General Motors written by one of its former executives, James Rinehart (1993), former president of GM, Canada, and before that, general manager of GM's Packard Electric Division:

> How was it possible in just twenty-two years for GM to have lost so much ground? It is worth a few minutes to identify the culprits. The root of the problem was that transfer prices from divisions like Packard Electric were kept above competitive levels by a deliberate policy of GM management. The result was enormous slack that was soon filled by rising costs, leading to the noncompetitive situation . . . in 1975. [p. 146]

Rinehart then refers to two related policies: one of "keeping internal profitability a secret," and the other, one "that pre-

vented the end-product division from outsourcing any product
made by a supplying division without corporate permission."
The result of all this

> was not only a loss of overall product cost competitiveness, but,
> even worse, a lack of knowledge of what domestic competitive
> levels actually were, and, beyond this, what was going on in
> Japan. In 1953 the fact that GM internally supplied 65% of its
> components as opposed to 50% at Ford and 35% at Chrysler, was
> seen as a competitive advantage because it was considered greater
> added value. But because the 65% "value added" actually con-
> sisted of inflated costs, by 1975 this supposed advantage had been
> transformed into a millstone around GM's neck in the eyes of
> price-conscious buyers and auto industry observers. [pp. 146–
> 47]

Most managers of "business units" within corporations do
not know what some of their important costs are. In particular,
they seldom know how much capital they employ and what the
cost of that capital is. Their cost of capital is usually hidden in
costs allocated to them from above. Undifferentiated allocated
costs are sometimes as high as 50 percent of the costs that a
unit can account for. How can managers reasonably be held
responsible for the profitability of their units when they neither
know nor can control a large portion of their costs? They don't
have the information needed to manage their units well. As I
will try to show, it is available in an internal market economy.

The macroeconomy of the United States involves relatively
(but not completely) autonomous competitive suppliers of
goods and services. Some regulation is required because,
among other things, these units do not have perfect information about the potential effects of their behavior. For example,
they may be unaware of how a sale abroad may conflict with
U.S. foreign policy, or how their disposal of waste degrades the
environment occupied by others.

Even when enterprises are aware of their effects on others,

they do not always behave ethically or in the best interests of either their stakeholders, their environments, or the systems that contain them. Whatever centralized control there is in a market economy is supposed to provide no more regulation than is required to enable the market to operate effectively from the point of view of the nation as a whole and to protect the interests of the stakeholders who lack the information required to evaluate what is or might otherwise be placed in the market. For example, the Federal Food and Drug Administration conducts evaluations of proposed foods and drugs that their potential consumers can't. Therefore, it can provide consumers with the information they need to act intelligently. In addition, even when consumers are aware of the potential harm associated with use of a supplier's product or service, they cannot always do something about it. The government can; it can prevent suppliers from engaging in activities that are harmful to consumers.

Macroeconomies versus Microeconomies

Why does the nation have one type of economy (market) but the organizations it contains have another(centrally planned and centrally controlled)? Some argue that this follows from the fact that the economic problems of a nation are of a different magnitude and complexity than those of companies. However, this is not so; for example, IBM, GM, and AT&T are among the largest economies in the world. According to an account published by *The Philadelphia Inquirer* (December 26, 1991) of a report published by The Conference Board, "Of the 100 largest economies in the world in 1989, 47 were corporations, not countries. . . . General Motors Corp. was not only the world's largest company, it was also the 20th-largest economic unit on the planet, beating out most of the world's 130-plus nations" (p. 12B). This is not a reason for organizing corporations and public institutions around internal market economies, but it is a reason for asking: What would happen if this were done? Would their performance be better or worse?

Internal Market Economies

With a few minor exceptions, for-profit and not-for-profit corporations operating with an internal market economy operate as profit centers. The difference between them lies in how their profit can be used, not in their need for it. Even not-for-profit organizations must concern themselves with profit unless they are protected by subsidizers. Similarly, with a few exceptions, units within corporations that have an internal market economy operate as profit centers. The only exceptions are units whose output cannot or should not be provided to any external user, usually for competitive reasons, or that have only one internal user. The corporate secretary, for example, serves the chief executive officer and no one else. For competitive reasons, it may not be prudent to allow a corporate planning department to carry out planning for other corporations. In such a case the department would be operated as a cost center with the executive office, which would be a profit center. (More on the executive office below.) A unit that produces a product whose composition is classified for competitive reasons would also not be expected to operate as a profit center. It would operate as a cost center that is part of a profit center. Every cost center should be part of a profit center. Such an arrangement is necessary, though not sufficient, to provide assurance that costs will be controlled.

It is very important to realize that not all profit centers are expected to be profitable, even though their profitability is taken into account in evaluating their performance. For example, a company may retain an unprofitable unit because of the prestige it brings to the parent (e.g., Steuben Glass to Corning) or because its product is sold at a very low cost as a loss leader. An unprofitable unit may also be used to produce a product or provide a service that is required to round out a product line or service line. One company whose wholesalers are either exclusive distributors of its products, or almost so, deliberately diversified into an unprofitable product line to provide its wholesalers with another product related to their main one and that they could expand into without reducing their attention to the primary product. This process has been in effect for more than ten years at a continuing cost to the company, but it has what is by far the most effective distribution system in its industry.

Subject to the minimal constraints (discussed below) that are imposed on profit centers to protect corporate interests, these centers should have the freedom (1) to buy any service or product they want from whatever source they want at whatever price they are willing to pay, and (2) to sell their outputs to whomever they want at whatever price they want or are willing to accept. Because some corporate units may lack relevant information about other corporate units, and, more importantly, because they may not understand all the complex interactions among units, they might not act in the best interests of the corporation as a whole. For example, an organizational unit that shifts to an external source of supply may discharge the only available technicians with the skills required by other organizational units to evaluate external suppliers. Higher-level units must be able to intervene when lower-level units fail knowingly or unknowingly to act in the best interests of the whole of which they are a part.

No part of a corporation can be justified as part of the corporation unless it contributes to the value of the corporation as a whole. On the other hand, a corporation is not justified in containing a unit to which it does not add value or that would have a higher value outside the corporation than within it. The value that a unit gains by being part of a corporation derives from its interactions with other units. Therefore, even in an organization that operates with a market economy it is reasonable to require internal units that want to outsource to give internal supplying units the opportunity to meet externally quoted prices. However, even if an internal supplier meets or goes under an externally quoted price, the internal buyer should still be free to select the external supplier for other than cost reasons—for example, because of the quality of products or services provided.

A corporation with an internal market economy must be able to intervene effectively in the buying and selling behavior of its parts, but it should do so only when this clearly benefits the corporation as a whole. This can be facilitated by restricting the types of intervention permitted and imposing a cost on them.

Executive Overrides

At times a corporate executive may believe that a purchase made by a subordinate unit from an external source (even if made at a lower price than an internal supplier would charge) would be harmful to the corporation. For example, it might lead to the loss of highly skilled personnel who would be extremely difficult, if at all possible, to replace. In such cases, the executive can require that the purchase be made from the internal supplier, but *that executive must pay for the difference between the internal and the external prices.* This means that the buying unit will *not* have to pay more than it would have had to pay had it been free to buy from the external source. In addition, since executives who override subordinate units will also be profit centers or parts of one, they will have to consider explicitly the benefits as well as the costs of such interventions. Therefore these decisions are not likely to be made arbitrarily.

Recall the case involving an executive vice president who consistently required one internal unit to buy small electric motors from another internal unit. These motors could often be obtained externally for less money. The company involved eventually converted to an internal market economy. When it did, the vice president had to pay for the restrictions he imposed on outsourcing. At the end of the year he had been charged several million dollars for his overrides. This forced him to compare this cost with the benefits he thought he had obtained. He found that he could not justify his expenditures. As a result, he decided to free the two units involved to buy and sell motors as they wanted the following year. Not only did the internal buying and selling units improve their financial performance, they also became friendly and cooperative, and the executive became more profitable and stopped feeling like the referee of a prizefight. The buying unit continued to use the motor manufacturing unit as its major source of supply.

When corporate executives believe that an internal unit's potential sale to an external customer is not in the corporation's best interests, they can override that sale, but only by providing the internal unit with the amount of profit it would have made from it. This means that a selling unit will not have its profits reduced when kept from making a sale, and it will never have to sell its output at a price lower than it wants to.

When managers believe that a particular kind of external purchase or sale should not be made *under any conditions*, they can act like a government relative to their subordinate units by establishing appropriate restrictive rules or regulations. For example, the federal government of the United States prevents the sale of certain (for instance, military) products to designated foreign countries (currently Iran and Iraq) because it considers such sales to be against national interests. Corporate managers may act similarly. For example, they may preclude use of an external processor to make a food product sold by the company because the product's formula is considered to be secret and of competitive value. Coca-Cola is not about to allow an external supplier to make Coke syrup for it.

Julio Bartol, former CEO of Armco Latin America, and Ali Geranmayeh (Bartol and Geranmayeh, 1993) gave other reasons for considering the possibility of not permitting a service function to operate as a business unit:

> [A] company cannot remain indifferent to the sourcing decisions of its internal units when they concern strategic components of the company's products. And it simply cannot rely on outside suppliers for development and provision of its core technologies. It is possible, of course, to secure such requirements through joint ventures with other suppliers, or through contracting proprietary research, but to completely rely on independent suppliers for such technologies would not be wise. [pp. 167–68]

Henry Pfendt (1993), formerly head of the corporate computing center at Kodak, created such alliances of Kodak with external suppliers. IBM manages the day to day operations of the North American Data Center which is a state of the art facility and into which six [Kodak] data centers have been consolidated. Digital manages the day to day operations of the global voice, data, networks. JWP Businessland handles all the North American P.C. Support Services of Software/hardware plus help desk and consulting.

Bartol and Geranmayeh went on to describe their decision not to permit the externalization of an internal service unit:

> We have developed quite an advanced capability to use our financial expertise in enhancing our overall strategy. A preliminary survey confirmed strong external demand for such financial services. The problem we confronted was whether we would be willing to convert our finance department into an enterprise that would compete for external business. And conversely, would we allow our operating companies to obtain financial services from external sources of their choice? We answered "no" to both questions despite the strong likelihood of attractive returns for a financial service business, and the unlikelihood that any operating company would find better service from an outside source. What helped us in making this decision was our idealized design, and the determination that finance was a core competency for us, and that we did not want to enter the financial services business.

Financial services simply did not fit within the design we had created for our company, and pursuing outside sales only on an opportunistic basis would be distracting to our core business. [p. 169]

In contrast, John P. Starr (1993), then president of Alcoa Separation Technology, wrote:

Under the old system, the only way the R&D group could fund projects was to convince a business unit that they had a great idea. As a result, the battles between R&D and business units became legendary. R&D always complained that the marketing groups were too short-term-oriented and did not understand the complexities of long-term development. Business units complained that R&D could never finish anything, was prohibitively expensive, and was always off working on some hare-brained idea rather than accomplishing projects that would yield revenue sometime in this century.

After the internal market was working, R&D was forced to do some serious reflection. Realizing that their internal customers had limited funds and desires for longer-term work, they decided to reorient themselves to focus on various hot projects emerging from the business units. This did not satisfy their interests in more creative and challenging projects, so they decided to search outside for funding from various clients that valued their special expertise. Certain boundaries were placed on this pursuit, primarily that any work they obtained must be linked to the strategic direction of the company.

As a result of these efforts, R&D has now moved to the point where almost 35 percent of its budget is being funded via external sources. They have done an exceptional job of finding funding for projects that contribute to our strategic goals, and even the business units have been pleasantly surprised by the new possibilities that have been introduced. [pp. 139–40]

The Executive Unit

As noted earlier, in corporations that have an internal market economy, executive officers and offices operate as profit centers. They incur costs when they override purchasing or selling decisions of subordinate internal units. They also incur other types of cost, for example, for externally provided consulting or staff services, for interest on money they have borrowed, for taxes and dividends, and for services they require—such as financial, accounting, and legal—that are supplied either internally or externally.

Executive units also have two major sources of income. First, they charge subordinate units for the operating and investment capital they provide. Subordinate units then know what capital they are using and pay for it at a cost related to the risk involved and its cost to the corporation. (Where a subordinate unit is set up as a wholly owned but separate corporation, it may be given the option of obtaining capital directly from external sources.) The second source of income to the executive unit is a tax it imposes on each unit. This tax should cover the operating cost of, and the taxes imposed on, the executive unit. Tax rates should be established in advance of the period in which they are to be applied, and with the participation of the taxed units—that is, there should be no taxation without representation. (The circular organization facilitates such representation.)

What happened to Clark Equipment's executive headquarters is an excellent example of what can occur when an executive unit becomes a profit center in a market economy. James Rinehart (1993), the CEO of Clark who lead this transformation, wrote of it as follows:

> On January 1982, when I came aboard, the number of people working within corporate headquarters was a shade under 500, burdening Clark Equipment with unneeded administrative overhead. Our first step was to identify possible free-standing businesses encompassed within the corporate office. The list included a law firm, an accounting firm, a trucking company, and a printing and graphics company. These units were given two years to become self-supporting by accomplishing two goals: (1)

develop 50 percent of their business outside Clark, and (2) earn their cost of capital.

After one year, Clark's operating companies were no longer required to use these internal services. If an internal service met the two objectives above, they had three options: (1) become a Clark operating company, (2) undertake an employee buyout, or (3) find themselves a new owner.

If they failed to meet the above two objectives, option 1 was not available to them. The result was three buyouts, one sale, and one new Clark operating company. . . .

The second step was to announce that the corporate personnel and purchasing staffs would be phased out in one year as the new operating companies assumed these responsibilities. . . . A few of them [the people on these corporate staffs] accepted offers from other companies, and the majority left under one or another of our voluntary separation plans. These two steps reduced the corporate office to less than 100, which resulted in a huge decrease in overhead costs. . . .

The third step was to redesign the working relationships between business units and the corporate office to minimize bureaucratic controls. For example, we developed a decentralized cost system that required no central office intervention and a corporate consolidation program that required only one corporate office person. . . . At this point, the corporate staff dropped to less than 75, and we began examining what might be considered the ideal future for the corporate office of a market-driven organization. [pp. 148–49]

Profit Accumulation

Each profit center should be permitted to accumulate profit up to a level set for that particular unit. (This level may vary by unit.) Profit up to this limit should be available to the unit for any use it desires as long as this use does not have an adverse effect on any other part of the corporation or the corporation as a whole. If it can have such an effect, approval is required of the units affected or the lowest-level manager to whom all the units affected report. Accumulations of capital in excess of the specified amount are passed up to the next higher-level of the organization for its use or for transmission to a still higher-level. A unit that provides its excess profit to a higher level unit is paid interest on it by that higher level unit at a rate that is no less than the lowest rate it must pay external sources of capital.

The purpose of the constraint on capital accumulation is to put "excessive capital" in the hands of units that can invest it profitably. (The units that generate it may not be able to do so.) Furthermore, it endows "cash cow" units with an importance they normally do not have because it becomes apparent that they provide the fuel for corporate growth and development. Any unit that believes it can profitably invest or use capital in excess of the limit imposed on it can apply for additional capital or a lifting of the limit of its accumulation to an appropriate higher-level unit.

Public Sector Applications

The use of an internal market economy is by no means restricted to private for-profit organizations. It can and has been used effectively in the public sector. For example, a centralized licensing bureau in Mexico City had a terrible record of inefficiency, corruption, and poor service. It was broken up into small offices in each section of the city. The income of each office was derived exclusively from a fee paid to it by the city government for each license it issued. (The amount varied by type of license.) Those wanting a licence could obtain it from any office. Unlike the one centralized bureaucratic monopoly that the new offices replaced, they could survive only by attracting and satisfying customers. Service quality increased, and service time, overall costs, and corruption decreased significantly.

A well-known example of an effort to introduce the market economy into the public sector is the proposed voucher system for supporting public schools that was developed by Christopher Jenks of Harvard University (1970) and publicized by Milton Friedman (1973). In this system the only income schools would receive would be obtained from their cashing vouchers turned over to them by parents of children who have applied to and been accepted by the school. Children and their parents could apply to any school they wanted. Parents would be supplied with the appropriate number of vouchers by local governments. The vouchers could also be used to cover all or part of the tuition required by private nonreligious schools.

The voucher system not only puts public schools into competition with each other, but it also makes them compete with private schools. Only those schools would survive that provide a service sufficiently valued by students and their parents to induce them to turn over their vouchers to them. This would convert the focus of public education from supplier to consumer.

It is worth noting that if schools operating in the voucher system are required to select among applicants at random, segregation in schools would not be possible. This can be modified by requiring schools to accept any applicant who lives within an area of responsibility assigned to them, and to select at random only from applicants living outside that area. The public school serving a specified area might be required to pay the transportation costs incurred by any students living within its area who have opted to attend a school in another area.

An internal market economy can be employed by many government service agencies, and to the extent that it is, the public's pressure to privatize these services might significantly decrease.

When services currently provided by government agencies—usually monopolistically—are turned over to the private sector, they frequently move into a market economy, with resulting increases in efficiency and responsiveness to consumers. An extended and provocative discussion of the possibility and desirability of such transformations is provided by E. S. Savas (1982).

Possible Objections

Proposals for the introduction of a market economy in an organization usually give rise to four major types of concern.

Accounting Requirements

First, skeptics argue that the additional amount of accounting required by such a system would be horrendous. Not true! The amount of accounting required is actually reduced. Most of the accounting and reporting currently required of organizational units are done to facilitate their control by higher-level units. In an internal market economy all that needs to be provided to higher-level units are the equivalent of a profit-and-loss statement and a balance sheet. Any additional information requested by a higher-level unit should be paid for by that unit. This has a strong tendency to reduce the amount of unnecessary information flowing within organizations. Most corporations suffer more from an overabundance of irrelevant information than a shortage of relevant information. (This thought is also expressed in Michael S. Scott Morton, 1991.) Furthermore, the amount of accounting required is reduced because the introduction of a market economy in a corporation generally leads to increased outsourcing, and because the amount of transactional information exchanged between internal suppliers and internal customers is generally much greater than the amount between internal customers/suppliers and external suppliers/customers.

Increased Internal Conflict

In any discussion of a market economy, the terms *conflict* and *competition* are bound to come into play. Unfortunately, they are often used interchangeably, but they are not the same thing. Conflict occurs when one party's gain is necessarily another's loss—in win-lose situations. Cooperation, of course, occurs when both parties win—in win-win situations.

Competition is conflict embedded in cooperation. Consider a tennis match between friends. They are in conflict with respect to winning the match. But this conflict serves a more important common objective with respect to which the players cooperate, recreation. In fact, the more intense the conflict—the tighter the match—the more cooperative they are with respect to their recreative objective.

Competition has sometimes been defined as conflict according to rules. The rules in competition are designed to assure the cooperation of the parties involved with respect to their, or a third party's, objective. The rules make the difference between a street brawl and a prizefight.

In economic competition two suppliers may be in conflict with respect to particular orders, but the customers involved benefit from that conflict, at least in principle. They are supposed to get higher-quality supplies less expensively as a result of the conflict between suppliers. Therefore, the conflict between suppliers is cooperative with respect to the customers. An internal market economy puts internal suppliers in competition with external suppliers for the benefit of internal customers.

John Charlton (1993) of Esso Petroleum Canada has made similar observations:

> There is a common perception that an internal market economy will decrease cooperation among business units, causing the organization to degenerate into an aggregation of people who do everything solely on the basis of their own interests.
>
> This perception is based on two assumptions that . . . are *"completely false."* The first false assumption is that cooperation does indeed exist in your organization today. If you look around, you may find that in many functionally oriented companies, cooperation is really minimum. Functions are rewarded for

functional excellence as opposed to their contribution to the goals of the larger organization. As a result each unit is a fiefdom in its own right. . . .

The second false assumption is that a commercial relationship is not a cooperative venture but a win/lose proposition. I think this perception is based on the "used-car salesman" model of what selling and buying is all about. Most professionals who are involved in marketing and selling today know that successful selling has become a win/win venture. . . . Any party trying to take advantage of the other will find itself without a contract. Win/lose relationships thrive in situations of unequal power (monopolistic internal suppliers). By breaking up monopolistic situations, internal markets can result in *better* cooperation, not worse. [pp. 201–2]

Most organizational units have much better relations with their external suppliers whom they are free to choose than they do with internal units whose services or products they are forced to use. Internal suppliers who must compete with external suppliers for internal customers' business are much more responsive to their internal customers than monopolistic suppliers.

For example, the corporate computing center of one very large corporation provided services to all units of the corporation without charge. Its costs of operation were covered by funds provided by corporate headquarters. These funds were obtained by overhead assessed to every corporate unit. The units using the corporate computing center complained continuously about the poor service they received and expressed the wish to use more responsive external services, and the internal units that did not use the center resented paying even indirectly for a service they did not use. The director of the computing center complained about the unreasonable demands made by users of his center. These conflicts led to the CEO asking that the output of the center be evaluated to determine whether it was worth its very high cost.

Heroic efforts were made to measure the value of the center's output, but they failed. The schedules of production operations, which constituted the major output of the center, were significantly modified by plant managers before they were applied, and no record was kept of their modifications. As a result, neither the impact on operating costs of the computer-generated schedules nor the modifications made to them could be estimated.

Because of this, the CEO decided to convert the computing center into a profit center whose services had to be paid for by using units at a price set by the center. In addition, internal units were allowed to use external services, and the center was permitted to sell its services to external customers at prices it set.

Within a few months, the number of computers in the center were reduced by a little more than a third. Nevertheless, it was doing almost all the work required by internal units, but now that internal units had to pay for their computing, the amount of it they requested was significantly reduced. Moreover, they were much more satisfied with the services they received because the center was more responsive to their needs. In addition, the center acquired a number of external customers whom it served very profitably. Not only did computing become an increasingly valuable strategic competence, but also the computing center earned a return on the investment higher than the average obtained by the corporation as a whole.

In another case, a diversified food manufacturer had a large market research unit that had a monopoly on corporate work. It was poorly regarded by most of the internal units that were required to use it; it was considered to be unresponsive to their needs and to offer an inferior quality of service. It, too, was converted into a profit center, with freedom to sell its services to whomever it wanted, and with the requirement that it become profitable within two years or else be eliminated. On the other hand, all its internal users were given freedom to obtain their market research wherever they wanted. Initially *all* of them moved to external suppliers. As a result, the internal unit in desperation began to look for external customers. It eventually succeeded, but only after significantly improving the quality of its services and reducing its cost. Within two years it had a thriving business. Internal units that had once used its services became curious about its external success and began to try it again. This time they found it responsive to their needs. Internal demand became so great that the unit had to reduce, but not eliminate, its external work. It did not have to sacrifice profitability to do so.

All or Nothing at All

A third argument used against an internal market economy is that it cannot be installed in part of an organization, only in the whole. Doing so may be difficult but not impossible. About three years ago KAD—Kodak's manufacturing arms that produces copy equipment, X-ray equipment, medical devices, cameras, and everything else but film—converted to an internal market economy. The first problem it faced derived from the fact that Kodak as a whole did not convert to an internal market economy. As a result, KAD had to operate as a market-oriented economy within a centrally planned and centrally controlled economy.

The corporation continued to allocate costs for services to KAD that could not break these charges down into those for services it used and those it didn't. Therefore it had to develop surrogate costs. It treated as a tax the estimated cost of corporately provided services it did not use. Furthermore, it had to continue reporting to the corporation as it had before converting to an internal market economy. Therefore it had to maintain two sets of books: one for the corporation and another for itself.

One year after its conversion, KAD's effectiveness had increased enough to make the corporation pay attention to it. Although the corporation did not convert to an internal market economy, it did make changes that enabled KAD to operate more easily with an internal market economy.

Like KAD in Kodak, the R&D unit of Esso Petroleum Canada (EPC) also converted to an internal market economy within a centrally controlled corporate economy, but in this case its containing unit (EPC) tried to facilitate the conversion. It did so because it considered the conversion to be a trial that, if successful, would induce it to support similar conversions of other units, and eventually of the whole.

Inability to Sell Externally

A fourth reason often given for not taking the idea of an internal market economy seriously is that certain internal service functions cannot "reasonably" be expected to obtain external customers. Accounting departments are often cited as an example. Nevertheless, Clark Equipment converted its accounting department into a profitable business unit. Many local small and medium-size companies lacked access to high-quality professional accountants and wanted such services badly. This enabled the accounting department to sell its services externally at a very good price. One consequence was that the quality of the services rendered to internal as well as external customers improved significantly; it had to in order to retain its customers.

Another company that occupied a number of buildings in a suburb of a major metropolitan area converted its facilities-and-services department (buildings, grounds, and utilities) into a profit center that operated within a corporate internal market economy. All of its internal users shifted to outside agencies from which they obtained better services at a lower cost than had been provided by the internal unit. As a result, the service department gradually shrank and was eventually eliminated, at a considerable saving to the company.

Advantages of an Internal Market Economy

A number of the benefits of an internal market economy have already been identified: in particular, increased responsiveness of internal suppliers, better quality and lower cost of internally supplied services and products, continuous rightsizing, elimination of fluff, debureaucratization, demonopolization, and so on. A few other advantages are worth mentioning.

First, because virtually every corporate unit operating within an internal market economy becomes a profit center, the same measures of performance can be applied to each of them. This makes it possible to compare performances of units that were previously not comparable—for example, manufacturing and accounting, and legal and buildings and grounds. On this point, John Charlton (1993) of Esso Petroleum Canada wrote:

> We want every member of our company to know how they can make the company more successful, and we want them to act on their knowledge. The profit orientation of the internal market facilitates this by providing alignment with the company's goal, and permitting measurement of the impact of each unit's performance on the bottom line. This measurement can and should be extended down through the corporation low enough for individuals to understand their own contribution. [p. 197]

Second, the manager of a profit center within an internal corporate market economy is a *general* manager of a semi-autonomous business unit. This provides all unit managers with opportunities to improve and demonstrate their general management skills. Therefore it enables executives to evaluate the general management ability of their subordinates better than they otherwise could.

Third, when units are converted to profit centers and are

given the autonomy that goes with it, their managers are in a much better position to obtain all the information they require to manage well. They become more concerned with providing themselves with the information they want than with providing their superiors with the information they want.

Conclusions

Conversion to an internal market economy is obviously not an easy task. Therefore it does not attract the fainthearted; it requires considerable courage and a good plan for conversion. John Charlton (1993) described one such plan:

> As we began to work with Research on an implementation plan, four elements emerged based on the learning from other companies. First, we had to work with the people in the organization to create a shared vision of what it would be like to operate in an internal market economy. This was done by redesigning the entire unit to operate in the new mode. Detailed business plans were drawn up for each of the units to give them specific performance targets and identify the activities they needed to do to be successful. This process provided answers to the key questions on people's minds: What does it mean to have an internal market economy? What do we do differently? What are the expected outcomes? And what are the expectations from us?
>
> Second, we involved our training department to address skill shortfalls, particularly in the area of business literacy. Third, we set up an operating framework for the internal market economy that included establishing formal contracts for all services so as to create a clear understanding of what is expected to be done for what price between the suppliers of services and their customers. We created timely reporting of results so there was quick feedback on performance. We also bridged the internal market system to the corporate accounting system, although we had clearly underestimated the level of effort involved. Lastly, we wanted to make sure we encouraged results by providing

recognition and reward for people when they did the right things. [pp. 200–201]

Conversion to an internal market economy can be risky for those managers whose units either are unable to compete effectively in the open market, or are no longer needed within the corporation. Such units are very likely to be eliminated. The fact that they should be eliminated offers little solace to those who are affected. The possibility of creating activities that will use excess personnel productively is seldom considered in such circumstances. Nevertheless, the managers who are responsible for the excess are often retained and moved to another unproductive activity. This is seldom the case for non-managerial personnel who are the victims of their managers' inefficiency.

A major obstruction to the conversion to an internal market economy is the reluctance of many higher-level managers to share with their subordinates information to which they alone have access. To be sure, information yields power over, and many managers are not willing to share such power. Internal market economies may decrease managers' power over, but they more than make up for this by increasing their power to. This is no consolation to those who value power over for its own sake and value it more than power to. Those who want authority for its own sake do not fit well into a democratic organization.

John P. Starr (1993), former president of Alcoa Separation Technology, wrote to this point:

> A market based economy operating on competition allows organizations and people to grow and mature. Just as we marvel at how nature can transform a weak, helpless child into a powerful adult able to protect its parents, so can small business units become strong internal enterprises able to strengthen the parent corporation as a whole. Our challenge as managers is to harness

those great reserves of energy laying dormant in people by turning them loose in a market-based enterprise system. [p. 142]

The installation of internal market economies in American corporations can provide them with an opportunity to increase their effectiveness by an order of magnitude. Such restructuring is as important to our country on the microeconomic level as it is to the parts of the former Soviet Union on the macroeconomic level. Without it they and we are destined to experience continued economic stagnation.

Chapter 6

The Multidimensional Organization

Because American corporations are now in a rapidly changing environment, they reorganize frequently. In fact, some appear to reorganize continuously. A great deal of time and energy are consumed in this process. In addition, the possibility of layoffs often associated with reorganization is very unsettling and frequently leads to decreased productivity. Little wonder, then, that reorganization is usually resisted, especially at the lower levels of an organization, where its effects are usually greatest.

Most institutions and enterprises seek what Donald Schon (1971) called a "stable state." Like a coiled spring, their resistance to change tends to be proportional to the pressure to change that is applied to them. The more turbulent their environment is, the more stability they seek. They do not realize that the only equilibrium that can be obtained in a turbulent environment is dynamic, like that of an airplane flying through a storm. However, reorganization is only one possible way of responding to environmental changes. If it were possible to design an organization that could adapt to change that affects it without reorganizing, then the resistance to change would be significantly reduced. Such an organizational design is possible. Its product is called a *multidimensional (MD) organization*.

All reorganizations consist of changing the relative importance of the criteria used in dividing labor. If units involving all three possible ways of dividing labor—by functions, products or services provided, or users supplied or served—are placed at each level of an organization, reorganization is never required. Then as the relative importance of these criteria change, all that is required is a reallocation of resources to existing units, not a change in structure. This requires explanation.

The MD Design

The MD concept was originally developed at Dow Corning by its board's chairman and CEO, William C. Goggin (1974). What is presented here is a significant variation on Goggin's theme. To understand how the design presented here eliminates the need to change the basic structure of an organization when faced with significant internal or external change, it is necessary to have a clear notion of what an organization is.

The need to organize derives from the need to divide labor. To organize is to divide labor and to coordinate it in such a way as to obtain a desired output. The more divided the labor, the more coordination is required. In a typical organization chart the horizontal dimension shows how labor is divided at each level—that is, how responsibility is allocated. The vertical dimension shows how labor at different levels is coordinated and integrated—that is, how authority is allocated.

There are only three ways of dividing labor, hence three types of organizational units:

1. *functionally defined (input) units,* the outputs of which are principally consumed or used internally—for example, purchasing, finance, legal, personnel, R&D, building and grounds, industrial relations, and parts manufacturing departments;

2. *product- or service-defined (output) units,* the outputs of which are principally consumed or used externally—for example, the Cadillac, Buick, Oldsmobile, Pontiac, and Chevrolet divisions of General Motors;

3. *market-defined units,* which are usually defined by the classification of external customers to whom they try to sell the outputs of product- and service-defined units; for example, units defined by the geographic areas they sell in, such as North and South America, Europe, Asia, and African divisions, or units defined by such categories of users as ultimate consumers, retailers, and wholesalers.

Organizations are normally designed from the top down, beginning with the chief executive officer (CEO) and sometimes a chief operating officer (COO). In designing the first level below the CEO and the COO, labor must be divided; hence one of or more of the three criteria must be used. At each successively lower level, labor is again divided, and therefore one or more criteria are used at each level. The higher the level at which a criterion is used, the more importance attributed to it by the organization. Therefore, the resulting organizational design always reflects the relative importance attributed to each criterion—function, product or service, and market. For example, in single-product companies, functional units are usually the most important; in multiproduct companies, product units are often the most important; and in multinationals, particularly those in fierce competition with other companies, market units defined by countries or regions are commonly the most important.

All reorganizations involve changing the relative importance of the three criteria used in dividing labor—that is, changing the levels at which units of the three types appear. For example, a reorganization takes place when a corporation whose senior vice presidents are defined by their functions— for example, personnel, finance, R&D, and so on—changes the definitions of the responsibilities of the senior vice presidents to ones involving coordination of activities in market areas—for example, North and South America, Europe, and so on. The functionally defined units are moved down the organizational hierarchy and now report to market-defined units, not to the executive office or officer.

Reordering the criteria used in an organization's design may be required by a change in its environment, in the organization itself, or in its role or function in the larger system of which it is part. A change in AT&T's environment occurred when it was deregulated and for the first time had to deal with such competitors as MCI and Sprint. This increased the relative importance of marketing and reduced that of functions as well as products and services. An increase in the number of products and their differences, such as occurs in diversification programs—for example, when PepsiCo acquired Frito-Lay and fast-food chains—may require elevating the importance of product-defined units. As a functionally-oriented or product-oriented company expands into foreign markets or increases the number of locations in which it has operations, it may have to convert to a market-oriented organization.

If units of all three types are established at a particular level of an organization (Fig. 6.1), then as their relative importance changes, all that is required is a reallocation of resources invested in their development. Reorganization is not required. If the three types of unit are established at every level of an organization, then the need to reorganize at any time is completely eliminated. Units of any of the three types can be added or subtracted without requiring reorganization; the organization's structure remains the same.

Figure 6.1 shows the three-dimensionality of the multi-

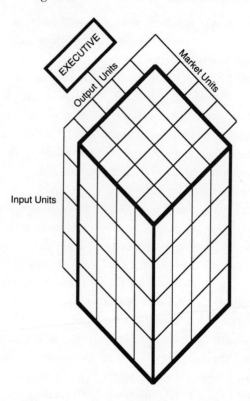

Fig. 6.1. A basic multidimensional design.

dimensional organization. The surface of each cube of which it is composed represents the intersection of two units of different types. Each cube represents the intersection of three units, one of each type. Not all units of an organization necessarily interact. Therefore, all intersections would not necessarily be operationally realized in a multidimensional organization.

The three-dimensional representation shown in Fig. 6.1 is not one most organizations like to use. Therefore, a representation such as is shown in Fig. 6.2 is more commonly used. A more conventional but less commonly used representation is shown in Fig. 6.3.

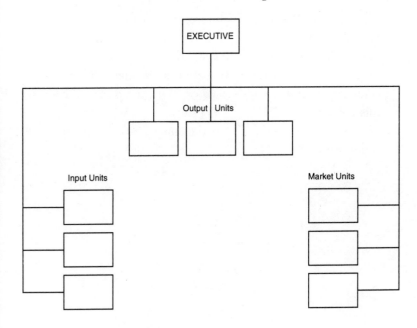

Fig. 6.2. Usual representation of a multidimensional organization.

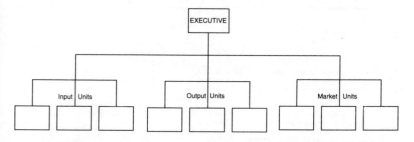

Fig. 6.3. Conventional representation of a multidimensional organization.

An Example

It may be helpful at this point to provide an example of a multidimensional organization to which reference can be made as we go into the details of the design. The example used here (and in Chapter 5) is that of Kodak's Computing and Telecommunication Services (CTS) Unit, which was subsequently dissolved into well-publicized joint ventures with **IBM, DEC,** and **JWP Businessland.** It should be borne in mind that every application of the multidimensional design is a variation on the theme presented here; no two are exactly alike. This will become apparent when additional examples are provided later in this chapter.

The description of CTS is the one prepared by the organization itself (Fig. 6.4).

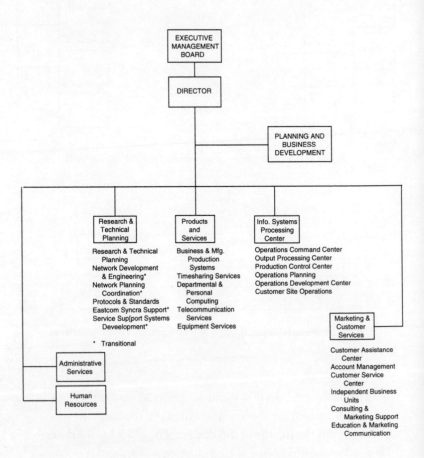

Fig. 6.4. Multidimensional design of CTS.

Groups and Output (*Product- and Service-Defined*) Units

- Each output unit within CTS will be responsible for improvements in its current line of products and services. Each unit may carry out its own research activity or buy such services from the Research and Technical Planning Group.

Research and Technical Planning Group

- This group will be the main research and development arm of CTS and will have responsibility for technology transfer to the operating units. The main objective of this unit will be to develop plans for products and services which will lead to addition of output units for CTS.
- This group will also assist the Executive Planning Board in development of strategic technical plans and architectures and provide prototyping or feasibility testing functions.
- This group will consist of two units: (1) Research and Technical Planning and (2) Protocols and Standards. Four other units will be assigned to this Group during the transitional period: Network Development and Engineering, Network Planning Coordination, Service Support Systems Development, and Eastcom Syncra Support.

Information Systems Processing Center

- This Group will be responsible for developing and operating the central computing, telecommunications, media storage facilities, and providing operational support for customer-owned facilities.
- This Group is composed of six units: Operations Command Center, Output Processing Center, Production Control Center, Customer Site Operations, Operations Development Center, and Operations Planning.

Products and Services

- This Group will have primary responsibility for the development, delivery, and support of the products and services offered by the organization. The Group comprises the following five units: Business and Manufacturing Production Systems, Timesharing Services, Department and Personal Computing Services, Telecommunication Services, and Equipment Services.

Market Units
Marketing and Customer Services

- This Group's primary responsibilities are to represent CTS to the customer and represent the customer to CTS. The organization will have the following functions:Account Management, Customer Assistance Center, Customer Service Center, Independent Consulting, Market Research facilitating competitive assessment, and Education and Marketing Communication. It will also nurture development of Independent Business Units.

Functional Units (Executive Support, Purchased or Provided)
Administrative Services

- Finance and Accounting, Purchasing, Legal, Directory, Computer and Telecommunication Security, and Assets Services.

Human Resources

- Will be responsible for facilitation of personnel planning, and developing and ensuring effectiveness of personnel policies within CTS. The administration of payroll and benefits will not be done in CTS.

Planning and Business Development

- Will be responsible for the coordination of all planning activities of CTS. This unit will serve in a staff capacity to the Executive Management Board and will conduct the necessary research and preparatory work for the Board's planning activities.

Executive Functions

- The Director will have responsibility for the performance of the unit as a whole, and have the following functions: (1) setting the guidelines for and principles of the operations of all subordinate units, (2) investing in the development of the units below, and (3) conducting financial, quality, and security audits of the units below.
- The CTS Executive Management Board will be responsible for strategic assessment of competitive opportunities on a worldwide basis. It may sponsor projects for evaluation of specific alternatives to facilitate formation of CTS standards and priorities.
- The Executive Management Board will create (and disband) ad hoc Councils as appropriate to facilitate its activities. Such Councils may include members who are external to the Board, or to the CTS organization.
- The Executive Management Board will have the following Councils: Business/Customer Advisory, Quality, Security, Technology, Human Resource, and Director's Council which will facilitate communications within CTS and address quality-of-work-life issues. It will be composed of members elected by the employees of CTS for terms not to exceed 12 months.

Functions and Functioning of Units

Although a multidimensional design can be used without an internal market economy, the value of each concept is greatly increased when the two are used together. Therefore this combination is assumed here, but it is easy enough to separate the two ideas and conceptualize the multidimensional organization independently of the internal market economy.

Product- or Service-Defined (Output) Units

In a multidimensional organization, product- and service-defined units consist of a management and a supporting staff, but no other personnel, and no facilities other than what is required to house this small number of people. (An exception is discussed below.) They make direct payments to all their internal or external suppliers for the services, facilities, and products they receive. Therefore they usually require no investment, since they have no fixed assets, but they do need operating capital.

Product- and service-defined units are responsible for all the activities required to make available and sell their products and/or services to customers. All of them are profit centers. They must buy all the inputs (goods and services) they require, and they are free to do so from either internal or external sources. This freedom is subject to such an override by a higher authority as was discussed in Chapter 5. Recall that the cost of an override is borne by the one who is responsible for it, not the one or ones affected by it.

Product- or service-defined units can pay an internal or external supplier on any basis they negotiate—for example, cost per unit, commission, fixed fee, or cost-plus. Although they have no control over their internal or external suppliers, they can influence them by use of their purchasing power.

These units obtain income from sale of their products or services. If they require more capital than they generate or accumulate, they can apply for it from a higher level of the organization. They are expected to treat such funds as loans or investments. They must pay for their use one way or another.

In an internal market economy, the profits that product- or service-defined units generate are subject to a tax levied by a higher level of management. The tax rate applied should be designated in advance of the relevant period. It should not be so large as to deprive profitable units of discretionary funds.

Ideally, the tax should be only large enough to cover the operating costs of the level of management that imposes the tax. Units should be able to use some of their profits as they see fit—for example, to improve old products, develop new ones, or open new markets. However, as discussed in Chapter 5, the accumulation of discretionary funds should be limited. Excessive accumulation of profit reflects an inability to find profitable uses for it. Therefore, excesses should be passed up to a higher level at which they can be used profitably.

Product- and service-defined units are easy to add or subtract because they usually have no fixed assets and they involve only a relatively small number of people. The exception occurs when such a unit is, and should remain, the exclusive user of an internal supplier of products or services. For example, a product-defined unit that is the only user of a manufacturing unit dedicated exclusively to supplying it, which, for competitive reasons, is not allowed to supply any potential external customers, should contain that manufacturing unit within it as a cost center. Whenever an internal unit has only one internal customer, and external customers are precluded for whatever reason, that unit should be part of the unit it supplies.

Functional (Input) Units

Functional units—that is, units that are functionally defined— provide goods or services most of which are used by other parts of the organizations, but they may also supply external customers. When they do more external than internal business, they should be treated as product- or service-defined units. Functional units provide such services as manufacturing, transportation, warehousing, data processing, personnel, legal, and accounting.

Some functional units need facilities and equipment as well as personnel to manage and operate them. Therefore these units may require investments as well as operating capital. As is the case with product- and service-defined units, functional units can apply to a higher level of the organization for more capital than they can generate or retain. Such investments or loans must be treated as though they were externally provided—that is, they must be payed for.

Like product- and service-defined units, functional units are profit centers in a multidimensional organization with an internal market economy and hence are evaluated in part by the amount of profit they generate and the return they provide on the investment made in them. They, too, are subject to a corporately imposed tax.

Functional units are free both to purchase whatever they need and to sell whatever they produce or provide, either internally or externally. Their purchasing and selling decisions are subject to intervention from above, and to compensation for such intervention when appropriate. They receive the income that their sales generate, and they pay the cost of whatever they purchase.

If an executive office believes that the external sales of a functional unit are expandable, even though they may be small at the time, it may create an output unit to promote such sales. For example, if an internal data-processing unit develops a substantial external business, the executive office may decide to create a data-processing service unit. Unless constrained from doing so by the executive office, the old data-processing functional unit can serve new external customers as well as old internal and external customers. The new external service unit may or may not use the internal service unit.

If the executive office observes that an important externally provided product or service is consumed heavily within the organization, it may create an appropriate functional unit or extend an existing one to provide that product or service internally. In general, it would do so only if it believes it can provide such a product or service with a quality superior to what it can get externally, or at a lower cost for an acceptable quality than it can get externally.

If a functional unit is used heavily by external but not internal consumers, a higher level of management should want to know why. Either the internal consumers are not purchasing wisely, or they no longer need the goods or services provided by that input unit. In the latter case, the input unit might either be converted to a product or service unit, or be sold or discontinued. On the other hand, the executive office should want to know why a functional unit that can satisfy an external demand makes little or no external sales.

The organization's structure need not be changed to accommodate either the addition or deletion of a functional unit.

Market (Defined) Units

Market units—that is, units defined by the markets they serve—have two functions. First, they sell the outputs of any other unit in the organization that wants to use their services. They are also free to sell their services externally, subject to the type of executive override discussed in Chapter 5. Second, they serve as advocates of the users in the markets in which they operate. They not only represent the company in the market, they also represent the market in the company.

Market units operate as profit centers that can generate discretionary funds. These can be used to initiate old-product improvements and new-product development. These developments may be sold internally or externally, subject to the usual executive override. Their income can be in the form of a commission on sales or fixed fees, or they may buy products from their internal or external producers and resell them at a profit.

In their advocacy role, market units evaluate the activities of other organizational units from the point of view of those outside the corporation who are, or can be, affected by them.

By calling together the heads of market units, the executive office or heads of other types of unit can obtain their users' evaluation of the company's performance over all the areas served, or in particular areas. This can help them identify unexploited opportunities and actual or potential threats. Therefore, market units can operate as consultants to the executive office and other unit heads. They should be paid for such service and be free to provide it to external noncompetitive organizations when doing so does not conflict with corporate objectives.

Because market units have few or no fixed assets, they can easily be added, subtracted, or otherwise modified.

Unit Designs

Many units in an MD organization can themselves be designed in three dimensions. Moreover, this can be done even when higher- or lower-level units have not been so designed. Fig. 6.5 shows how the Ministry of Health was organized in Iran shortly before the revolution. (It was one of the few branches of the government that was not reorganized after the revolution.) The country was divided into regions, and each was given a multidimensional organization of the type described above. However, the headquarters, consisting of the minister, his deputy ministers, and the regional directors, was organized conventionally.* In general, geographically distinct multidimensional units can be created where the regions are at least partially autonomous from a political point of view. For example, in a multinational corporation, national units may be organized multidimensionally even if the corporation isn't.

In research-and-development organizations, programs consisting of two or more projects have been organized multidimensionally, with their projects set up as output units, and skill groups as input units. However, such programs have reported to conventionally organized top managements. For ex-

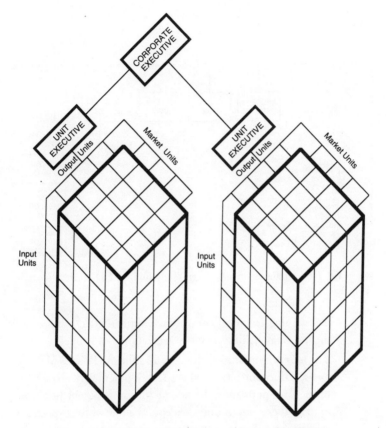

Fig. 6.5. A multidimensional design at the subunit level.

ample, a software producing research and development unit that is part of a large research organization is organized as shown on Fig. 6.6. This organization develops, installs, manages, services, and educates users and operators of large computer software systems.

- The Director is responsible for leading (1) a participation formulation of a vision, (2) generation of a shared image of a desired future, and (3) efforts to achieve the organization's mission. He also has final responsibility for obtaining and

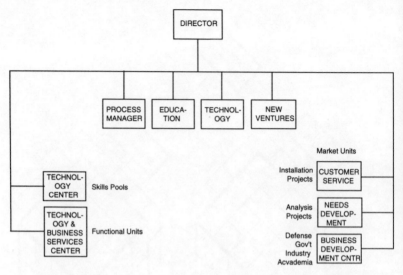

Fig. 6.6. Multidimensional design of a software R&D organization.

maintaining technical competence, human effectiveness, and the financial viability of the organization as a whole.

- The four output units of this organization are Process Management, Education, Technology Development, and New Ventures. The permanent homes of the professional personnel used by these output units, except for a few whose expertise is relevant to only one output unit, are the skill (input) units. Output units can, at exceptional times, hire or develop a scarce and broadly needed expertise; however, these experts are transferred to skill units in the Technology Center as soon as practical.

- The output units may initiate marketing activities addressed to customers who are exclusive to them, but they keep the Business Development Center informed and arrange a transition of their marketing activities to the Business Development Center unless the activities are short term or only for cost recovery. Marketing services addressed to customers of two or more output units are integrated and managed at the Business Development Center.

- The new Venture unit houses basic research and experimental efforts intended to give new and promising ideas a chance to develop and become marketable. When they do, they are either transferred to another output unit, or a new output unit is created to house them. The New Venture unit is also responsible for feasibility studies.

- There are two input units: the Technology Center and the Technical and Business Services Center. The former is responsible for the development of internal technical capabilities, and for ensuring that the reservoir of expertise in all relevant disciplines is ready, willing, and able to contribute to the output units. This Center may engage in internally generated projects in order to develop internal capabilities. Personnel in this Center are primarily engaged in output-unit projects, but they spend up to 20 percent of their time in their Skill Units for personal development.

- The Technical and Business Services Center provides the usual types of support services required by a research and development organization, for example, personnel administration; accounting; information management; procurement; space management and scheduling; library, computing, video studios, and telephone center; events planning and customer support; and administration of other shared services provided by outside sources.

- Finally, there are three market units: the Customer Service, Needs Development, and Business Development Center.

- The Customer Service Center has responsibility for software design and packaging to meet user requirements, and management of software installations.

- The Needs Development Center has two primary functions: to identify and develop specific customer needs, and to improve customer planning.

- The Business Development Center is divided into subunits serving Defense, Government Agencies, Industry, and Academia. It is responsible for consolidating and interpreting customer needs (helping customers understand their real needs), customer advocacy, business development and strategic planning, sales planning, prospecting and sales, and monitoring customer satisfaction.

The multidimensional structure can sometimes be applied at even the lowest organizational level. For example, a graphic reproduction unit can assign functions such as purchasing and billing to individuals, operation of different reproduction equipment to different individuals, and marketing of its services to one or more of its members. Several different functions can be assigned to a single individual. If such a unit is additionally managed as a profit center, it can be relatively autonomous.

Every unit in an MD organization can be organized in the same way as the organization as a whole is. This is most apparent in the case of functional units, particularly manufacturing. Functional subunits of a manufacturing unit might include purchasing, stores, maintenance, quality control, and so on. A manufacturing unit that sells parts and component production, subassembly, and assembly may organize service units accordingly. Its market subunits can be organized to match its internal and/or external customers. An example of a multidimensionally designed functional (manufacturing) unit of a large corporation is shown in Fig. 6.7.

In an MD organization with an internal market economy any function that a unit does not want to provide itself, it can purchase from other units, internal or external. For example, a functional unit such as data processing may want to buy its financial services from a financial unit that is also functionally defined.

In the limiting case, two or more multidimensional units can share all or some of their subunits along one dimension (Fig. 6.8).

Product and service units can be divided into product and service subunits using—for example, brands, models, or sizes

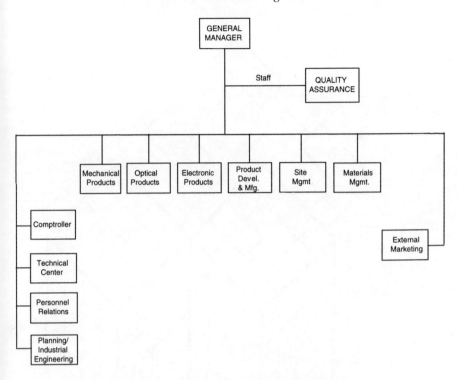

Fig. 6.7. Multidimensional design of a manufacturing division.

to define them. If large enough, such units can use one or several persons to take charge of acquiring and controlling each input they require, for example, manufacturing, transportation, and sales. These persons provide liaison with the supplying units.

Service subunits of a market unit can be defined by subdivisions of the area involved—for example, states or regions of a country. Functional subunits might include market research, media purchasing, special events specialists, and so on. Finally, since a marketing unit in an internal market economy can have external users, it may itself have a marketing activity that has responsibility for selling its services.

Although multidimensional design can be applied at any

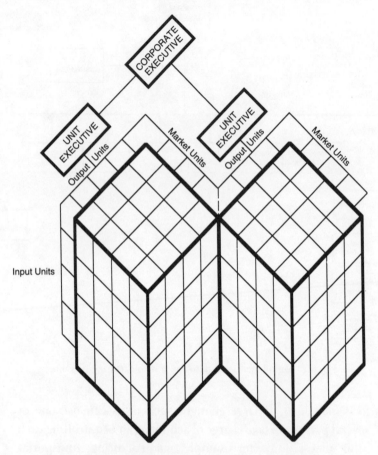

Fig. 6.8. Two multidimensional units with a common dimension.

level of an organization, in practice it has tended to be employed primarily at the upper level of organizations or in semi-autonomous business units.

Multidimensional Design of Large Organizations

If the number of units of any one type is too large to report directly to the chief executive, one or more coordinating executives can be used for each dimension (as shown in Fig. 6.9). The heads of the groups in the CTS design are essentially coordinators of a number of units. If the number of units in any one dimension is too large for one coordinator, more than one coordinator can be used. For example, functional units may be divided into two groups—operations and services—or, as in the CTS case, into Administrative Services and Human Resources. Product units may be divided into broad product categories such as automobiles, trucks, buses, and tractors or, as in the CTS case, Research and Technical Planning, Products and Services, and Information Systems and Processing Center. Markets can be grouped geographically and marketing activities can be claissified functionally—for example, in the CTS case, into Customer Assistance Center, Account Management, Customer Service Center, and so on.

Coordinating executives may be incorporated into the executive office.

MD vs. Matrix Organizations

Those familiar with matrix organizations will recognize their superficial resemblance to the multidimensional design presented here. Davis and Lawrence (1977), who are prominent proponents of the matrix, refer to multidimensional organizations as merely an expansion of a matrix form of organization (p. 234). Not so.

Davis and Lawrence wrote:

> We believe that the most useful definition [of the matrix organization] is based on the feature of a matrix organization that most clearly distinguishes it from conventional organizations. That is its abandonment of the age-old precept of "one man—one boss'" or a single chain of command in favor of a "two-boss" or multiple command system. So we define matrix as any organization that employs a multiple command system that includes not

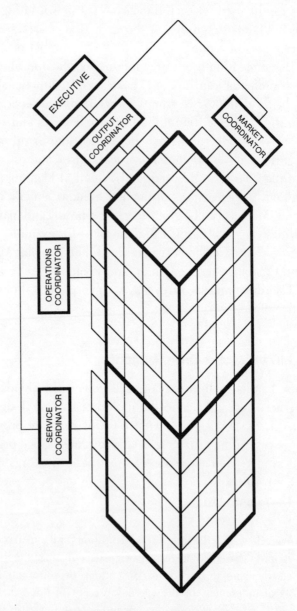

Fig. 6.9. A multidimensional design with coordinators.

only a multiple command structure but also related support mechanisms and an associated organizational culture and behavior pattern [p. 3].

The principal difference between MD and matrix organizations lies precisely in the fact that in matrix organizations employees have two bosses. One is the head of the input (support or staff) unit of which they are a part; the other is the head of the output (line) unit to which they are assigned. According to Jay Galbraith (1973), "They jointly determine his chances for promotion and his salary increase, and they determine performance goals with him." And later, "[T]he matrix design institutionalizes an adversary system" (p.105). This property of the design produces what might be called "organizational schizophrenia." When an employee's bosses do not agree or have different value systems, the employee does not know how to behave. This can be very stressful. The decision regarding to whom to pay attention is usually made politically rather than in the best interests of the organization. The multidimensional design creates no such problem.

In a multidimensional organization, members of one unit whose services have been purchased by another unit are related to the head of the second unit as they are to an external customer. They have only one boss, the head of the unit of which they are a part. The head of the unit for which they are working is their client, not their boss. Their boss may or may not use the client's evaluation of the server in evaluating the server. Those in one unit of an organization who work for another unit in that organization—for example, a computer programmer who writes a program for another part of the organization—know who their boss is and who their customers or clients are. Because it is much easier for a dissatisfied customer or clients to dismiss an unsatisfactory server than for a boss to dismiss an unsatisfactory subordinate, servers tend to be very responsive to those served, particularly when they are paying the unit of which the server is a part for the work. The responsiveness of servers can be encouraged by making their compensation reflect the amount of their time that is billable to customers or clients.

Furthermore, matrix organizations normally have only two dimensions—inputs and outputs—but not market units. If marketing is a separate function in a matrix organization, it is either incorporated in output units or set up as an input unit.

If marketing is organized as a functional unit rather than on a third dimension, the result is a two-dimensional organization, not a matrix, because employees do not have two bosses, and most units are profit centers. The elimination of the market dimension may reduce organizational flexibility and sensitivity to the needs and desires of customers and consumers. In particular, it eliminates the role of marketing personnel as advocates of the customers and consumers. However, there are situations in which marketing is clearly best done by those who produce the product or service offered to the outside world. This was the case for ALAD (Armco's Latin American Division).

This metal-producing business unit, a subsidiary of Armco, a multinational company, operated in eight different countries. Its design was two-dimensional because it incorporated marketing into its product (output) units. It did so because of the substantial amount of technical content of its products and the desire of its customers to have direct contact with the producers of the products they bought. ALAD's design is shown in Fig. 6.10, which also shows the company's explanatory notes. This organization also adopted an internal market economy and circular organization.

Since matrix organizations are seldom endowed with internal market economies, their functional units are usually subsidized and therefore often tend to become bureaucratic monop-

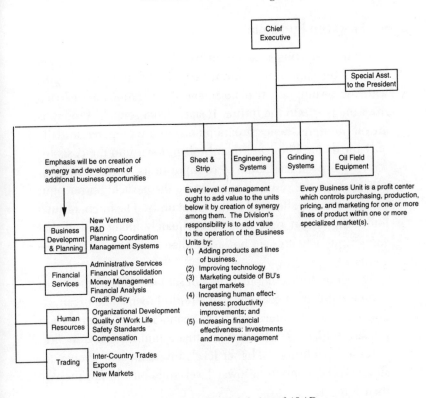

Fig. 6.10. Multidimensional design of ALAD
(Armco's Latin American Division).

olies that are more interested in their own survival than in service to the organization of which they are a part. Their users seldom have alternative sources of supply, and they seldom have users outside the organization. Furthermore, because product and service (output) units in a matrix organization can have large investments in facilities and equipment and large complements of personnel, they are much more difficult to add to and subtract from a matrix organization than output units in a multidimensional organization. Recall that the latter usually include little but management and operating capital.

Program Budgeting

Program budgeting is a way in which managers can prepare budgets for subordinate input and output units and begins with the assumption that no financial obligations are carried from the past into the future. It starts from scratch. Programs are output units; hence program budgets are prepared initially only for them. These are then broken down into the costs for services or products required of input units. Input-unit budgets are then the result of aggregating the parts of output-unit budgets that are allocated to the input units. The intent of such budgeting is that programs be adequately financed and that supporting activities be no larger than required by the programs.

Program budgeting may be, but seldom is, associated with an internal market economy. In a multidimensional organization that has an internal market economy, managers do not prepare budgets for their subordinate units. Each unit prepares its own budget. Higher levels invest in, lend money to, and extract money from lower-level units but do not prepare their budgets.

Program budgeting normally does not affect organizational design (although it is more compatible with matrix organizations that with traditional ones), and it has no effect on organizational flexibility. Such budgeting does make it easier to eliminate "make work" and estimate the financial requirements of both output and input units, assuming that the output units must use the input units as their sources of supply. Therefore, program budgeting does nothing by way of benchmarking input activities; it provides no comparison of internal costs with those that would be incurred by using external sources of supply. Internally provided support services may well be excessively costly without this being revealed by the budgeting procedure. In an MD organization with an internal market economy, every input unit competes against external sources of their outputs. Therefore, in such an organization benchmarking is automatic and continuous.

Conclusion

Many if not most of the obstructions to change are either removed or significantly diminished in a multidimensional organization operating within an internal market economy. First, in such an organization there is no need to reorganize in order to change the relative importance of criteria used in dividing work. Emphasis can be changed by reallocation of resources and by the imposition of constraints by higher levels of management.

Second, units can be added, subtracted, or modified without serious dislocation of other units. The more internal and external customers an internal unit has, the more robust it is and the less dependent it tends to be on any one customer.

Third, lower-level managers are given as much autonomy and general management experience as higher-level managers because even low-level units are operated as complete businesses within a market economy. Because higher-level managers also manage profit centers, they must take full responsibility for the effects of their decisions on the performance of units they oversee. Their primary concern must be with how their subordinate units interact with each other and how they interact with other parts of the organization and its environment, not their actions taken separately.

Last, a uniform, explicit, and operationally unambiguous measure of performance that incorporates some function of the amount of profit generated—for example, return on capital employed—can be applied to units at every level, including the executive office. This makes possible comparison of the performances of units at all levels and discourages "make work" and bureaucracy. However, profit is not the only important performance characteristic. Recall that in a social-systemically conceived organization, development of the organization, its stakeholders, and its containing systems is its overriding objective. Although profit is necessary for corporate development, it is not sufficient.

When every part of an organization is organized multidimensionally, the organization can be said to be a *fractal*. Fractals are entities whose structure is the same at each of its levels. In view of the fact that fractals are currently making possible major advances in our understanding of nature, one would think that fractal organizations would attract the attention of social scientists, but not so. Because comprehensive MD organizations operating with internal market economies are fractals, every manager within them is a general manager no matter how specialized their unit may be. Each manages a complete business. Their differences are largely of scale. This characteristic of MD organizations simplifies succession planning and management development.

Finally, the circular organization, the internal market economy, and multidimensional design can all be combined in one organization. The power of each is significantly enhanced by its interactions with the others.

Epilogue

New Business Education

The transformations of corporations discussed in the preceding chapters clearly require informed, if not inspired, leadership. Unfortunately, we cannot look to business schools to provide the required leaders. These schools are bastions of dynamic conservatism that submit to only the minimal changes required to maintain the illusion of their relevance. They become less and less relevant as the rate of change in, and complexity of, the global economy and society at large increases. Their graduates are virtually useless upon graduation. Therefore, the length of time required of their first employers to educate them up to a state of usefulness keeps increasing.

Professor Noel Tichy is reported by Muller, Porter, and Rehder (1991, p. 83) to have said: "Business education is a disaster and needs radical transformation." Kamal N. Saad (1984) had noted earlier that "To the business community, the university is irrelevant to the real world. It is remote from reality" (p. 3). Japanese executives, when asked whether they are apprehensive about a resurrection of the American economy, have on a number of occasions said "no." When asked why not, they have said that as long as American managers continue to be educated in business schools, the Japanese have nothing to worry about.

Because the Harvard Business School is generally considered by many to be the best of its type, it receives the brunt of the criticism. Therefore, the criticism it receives is even more applicable to the many business schools that try desperately to imitate it. Keeping this in mind, consider some of the criticism to which the Harvard Business School had been subjected. The humorist Art Buchwald is reported to have written in 1973 that "[The] real villain of the oil crisis is the Harvard Business School. . . . Almost every Arab sheik now in charge of his country's oil policy was trained at Harvard." This sentiment was echoed by Peter Drucker: "Harvard, to me, combines the worst of German academic arrogance with bad American theological seminary habits. . . . The great trouble with a Harvard-type program is the arrogance it breeds. Students do not learn how difficult it is to accomplish anything."

Robert Townsend (1970) echoed these sentiments:

> Don't hire Harvard Business School graduates. This worthy enterprise confesses that it trains its students for only three posts—executive vice-president, president, and board chairman. . . . This elite, in my opinion, is missing some pretty fundamental requirements for success: humility; respect for people on the firing line; deep understanding of the nature of the business and the kind of people who can enjoy themselves making it prosper; respect from way down the line; a demonstrated record of guts, industry, loyalty down, judgment, fairness, and honesty under pressure. [pp. 53–54]

Dealing with business schools generally, Robert J. Samuelson (1990) wrote:

For three decades we've run an experiment on the social utility of business schools. They've flunked. Between 1963 and 1987 the annual number of MBA graduates [in the United States] rose from 5,787 to 67,496. There are now more than a million MBAs. If they were improving the quality of U.S. management, the results ought to be obvious by now. They aren't. Indeed, the MBA explosion has coincided with a deterioration in the performance and stature of corporate America. [p. 49]

Dobyns and Crawford-Mason (1991) report that in an interview the eminent pollster Daniel Yankelovich said, "I think that the business schools were responsible for some of the worst things that happened in American business, some of the short-term financial orientation, and, therefore, they ought to take responsibility for reversing it" (p. 88).

Furthermore, much of what business school students are taught in classes is incompatible with the world in which they eventually have to earn a living. As Peter Drucker observed, "In business school classrooms they construct wonderful models of a nonworld." Therefore, many graduates of these schools are not prepared to cope effectively with the real world.

It seems to me that the two principal effects that business schools have on students are (1) to provide them with a vocabulary that enables them to speak authoritatively about subjects they do not understand and (2) to induce them to accept and propagate principles that have demonstrated their ability to withstand any amount of disconfirming evidence.

Some Business School Deficiencies in Detail

Many of the deficiencies of business schools are deficiencies of formal education in general, education of all types at all levels. Nowhere is the truth of Marshall McCluhan's message (1964) "The medium is the message" so clear as in educational processes. Much (if not most) of what students learn in schools is derived from the nature of the educational process, the medium, rather than from the messages delivered through that process.

Most schools are industrialized disseminators of information and knowledge. They have little to do with the generation or spread of understanding and wisdom. They use materials and methods that would be appropriate if students were black boxes whose output hopefully exactly matched what was put into them earlier. What most educators expect of most students can be done better by computers and recording machines, and students know this. Computers can remember and recall, compare, and calculate more quickly than human beings can. But they cannot forget as easily as people can. Teachers forget that forgetting what is irrelevant is at least as important as remembering what is relevant. Students do not want to be put into competition with machines or treated as adjuncts to them; they want to do what machines cannot do, getting help from the machines to do so.

Students cannot learn how to go beyond what machines can do in a system that treats them like a product to be worked on and put together on an assembly line called a "curriculum." Their processing on this line is increasingly performed by machines: registration, billing, grading papers, performance reporting, playing computer-based games, and computer-assisted instruction. Their concept of self cannot help but suffer from being taught by a machine that the system tells them knows more than they do.

Most schools are unconsciously modeled after factories. Incoming students are treated like raw material coming onto a production line that converts them into a finished product. Each step in the conversion process is planned and scheduled, including work breaks and quality testing. Few concessions are made to the animated nature of the material processed. Although the raw material varies widely in quality, its treatment is uniform. The production process is considered to be successful if the final product is in high demand and can be sold at a high price. The system even puts brand names and model numbers on its products.

Formal education at all levels has been reduced to a number of discrete and disconnected parts. They have dissected teaching—not learning—into schools, curricula, grades, subjects, courses, lectures, lessons, and exercises. Pseudoquantification and pseudoqualification are used to reflect the system's concept of the amount and level of what has been learned: grades, credits, diplomas, and degrees. Formal education is seldom if ever treated in a unified way, synthetically; nor is it thought of by educators as part of a larger learning process, most of which takes place out of school.

Unless students *unlearn* a great deal of what they learned in school, they are seriously handicapped. Consider the nature of some of these handicaps.

Problems, Exercises, and Questions

Throughout their formal education students are evaluated by their ability to solve problems given to them. Therefore it is not surprising that they go out into the real world assuming that problems will continue to be given to them. They are in for a rude awakening. Problems are seldom *given* to those who have finished with school one way or another; they usually have to be *taken*, extracted from complex situations. However, most students are not taught and do not learn how to identify problems and formulate them effectively. Nevertheless, there is an old adage to the effect that a problem well formulated is at least half solved. Students, particularly business students, do not learn that the wrong solution to the right problem is generally worth more than the right solution to the wrong problem. The first type of error is easier to identify and correct, hence is more likely to induce learning.

Problems are not out there waiting to be taken, like apples

off a tree. They are abstractions extracted from reality by analysis. They are to reality what atoms are to such objects as tables and chairs. What we experience are tables and chairs, not atoms; similarly, what we experience are complex systems of interacting problems, not individual problems. This is why they have to be formulated. If they were real and ready-made like apples, all we would have to do is pick them.

Problems are situations in which one or more decision-makers can select from among alternative courses of action that are producers of outcomes of different values to the decision-maker or decision-makers. Since the values of the possible outcomes depend on the context within which they can occur, problem formulation requires knowledge of that context as well as the choices and their possible outcomes. Put another way: Problems are choice situations in which what is done "makes a significant (value) difference" to the decision-maker.

Exercises are abstractions of abstractions, problems from which at least some of the information required to formulate them properly has been omitted. However, the reason for wanting to solve the problem from which the exercise is abstracted is provided. *A question is an exercise from which even the reason for wanting to solve it and information about its context have been omitted.* Their differences are revealed by examples.

Most of what teachers consider to be problems are not problems at all; they are exercises or questions. Since few teachers are aware of the differences among problems, exercises, and questions, let alone the significance of these differences, even fewer students are aware of them.

First, consider an example of the conversion of a problem into an exercise. I was once given the following alleged problem by a friend. "You dip into a bowl containing black and white balls and pull out m balls of which n are black, hence $(m - n)$ are white. Now if, without replacing the balls you have drawn from the bowl, you dip into the bowl and pick one ball at random, what is the probability that it will be black?" I told him I would answer his question if he told me how he knew the bowl contained only black and white balls. He responded by telling me that providing the information I requested would spoil the problem. The fact is that he had already spoiled it; it was not a problem but an exercise. He had omitted information on how he, or someone else, had determined that the bowl contained only black and white balls. Such information could not help but be relevant in estimating the probability asked for by my friend.

The case studies widely used in teaching management are exercises, not problems. Their formulation leaves out much of the information required to formulate them. To be sure, the cases presented to students contain all the information that their authors consider to be relevant, and they leave out all the information the authors consider to be irrelevant. However, they do not reveal the criteria used to differentiate relevant from irrelevant information. These criteria are very relevant in problem-solving. Good problem formulations and solutions often involve discovering that information considered to be irrelevant by one party is very relevant to another. For example, I was once confronted with the following problem by a consultant who was having difficulty solving it.

A large city in Europe uses double-decker buses for public transportation. Each bus has a driver and a conductor. The driver is seated in a compartment separated by glass from the passengers. The closer the driver keeps to schedule, the more he is paid. The conductor collects zoned fares from boarding passengers, issues receipts and collects them from disembarking passengers, then checks them to see that the correct fare has been paid. He also is supposed to signal the driver when the bus is ready to move on after stopping to receive or discharge passengers. Passengers who want to disembark at the next stop signal the driver by pulling an easy-to-reach cord. Undercover inspectors ride the buses periodically to determine whether conductors collect all the fares and issue and check all the receipts. The fewer misses they observe, the more the conductors are paid.

To avoid delays during rush hours, conductors usually let passengers board the buses without collecting their fares, which they subsequently tried to collect between stops. Because of crowded conditions on the buses, conductors could not always return to the entrance to signal the driver when to move on after a stop. This required the driver to determine when to do so by using his rearview mirror and determining when no one else was disembarking. This resulted in delays that were costly to the driver. As a result, hostility developed between drivers and conductors, and this led to a number of violent episodes.

The two unions representing drivers and conductors would not accept management's suggestion that the incentive payments be discontinued. They also rejected a subsequent proposal that the drivers and conductors share equally their combined incentive payments. The consultant who presented the problem to me had tried several times to bring representatives of the opposing sides together for a discussion that he had hoped would produce a resolution to the problem. Each such occasion had ended in a fight.

After describing this situation to me, the consultant asked if I had any idea how the problem might be solved. I said I hadn't but that I did have some questions. The first was: How many buses operate in the system at peak hours? He told me this was irrelevant, since the problem arose on each bus as a separate unit. I persisted, and eventually he gave in; he took me to his files, from which we learned that about 1,250 buses operated at peak hours. He asked me what good it did to know this. Since I didn't know, I ignored his question and asked another question: How many stops are there in the system? He showed great annoyance at this apparently irrelevant question but again indulgently returned to his files to find the answer: about 850 stops. This meant that during rush hours there were more buses operating than there were stops in the system. Therefore I suggested that conductors be taken off the buses at peak hours and placed at the stops. There they could collect fares from people who were waiting for buses, check the receipts of all those coming off buses, and always be in position to signal the drivers when it was safe for them to move on. (This is exactly what conductors on British trains do.)

The number of conductors required at peak hours was significantly reduced. This made it possible to have all conductors and drivers work a continuous eight-hour shift per day instead of a number of them working two four-hour shifts that were separated by off-peak hours.

What appears to be irrelevant information to one person may well turn out to be the key to the solution found by another.

The principal difference between excellent and ordinary organizational diagnosticians does not lie in the differences in the diagnoses they infer from the same information, but in the questions they ask to obtain additional relevant information. The information they obtain through their additional questions reduces the probability of an incorrect diagnosis.

Some management educators would argue that what is learned in dealing with cases, even if they are exercises, is useful in dealing with problems. This is like arguing that learning how to box with one hand tied behind one's back is useful in learning how to box with both hands. In boxing, skill depends on the way one's hands interact, not on how each operates independently of the other. In dealing with problems, skill depends on the way different mental operations interact— for example, right and left brain—not on the actions of each taken separately.

A question is a further abstraction from a problem; it is an exercise from which the reasons for wanting to solve it and its context are not revealed. In other words, a question is an unmotivated exercise, a problem completely out of context.

However, the reasons for wanting to answer a question determine what constitutes the right answer. For example, the correct answer to "How many finished products are in storage?" depends on the use to which the answer will be put. Is a product that requires repair to be counted? If the reason for asking the question is to determine how many items can be shipped to customers right now, items needing repair or parts should not be counted. If the items can be shipped within a week, then items that can be repaired within that time should be counted.

Even the question "How much are 2 plus 2?" has no meaning out of context. The answer will not be the same if the "2" refers to degrees Fahrenheit as it would be if it refers to chairs. Two plus 3 on a logarithmic scale is 6, not 5; 10 + 10 is 100 on the binary scale, and so on. To learn how to answer questions is not even to learn how to deal with exercises, let alone problems.

Problem Treatments

Business students are seldom made aware of the fact that in the "real world" there are four very different ways of dealing with a problem:

1. *Absolution:* to ignore a problem and hope it will solve itself or go away of its own accord.
2. *Resolution:* to do something that yields an outcome that's good enough, that "satisfices." This involves a clinical approach to problems that relies heavily on past experience, trial and error, qualitative judgment, and so-called common sense.
3. *Solution:* to do something that yields the best possible outcome, that "optimizes." This involves a research approach to problems, one that often relies heavily on experimentation, quantitative analysis, and uncommon sense.
4. *Dissolution:* to redesign either the entity that has the problem or its environment in such a way as to eliminate the problem

and enable the entity involved to do better in the future than the best it can do today—in a word, to "idealize."

The differences among these treatments are illustrated by the bus example used above, the one arising out of the conflict between drivers and conductors. Management initially tried to *absolve* itself of the problem by ignoring it and hoping it would go away. It didn't; things got worse. Next, management tried to *resolve* the problem by retracting the incentives, thereby returning to a previous state. However, the drivers and conductors rejected withdrawal of the incentives because it would have reduced their earnings. Management was unwilling to make up the difference because it expected productivity to decrease with withdrawal of the incentives. Then management tried to *solve* the problem by proposing that the driver and conductor on each bus share equally the sum of their incentive payments. This, management thought, would force drivers and conductors to cooperate. However, they rejected this proposal because they did not trust each other and therefore were unwilling to increase their interdependence in any way.

Recall that the problem was eventually *dissolved* by taking the conductors off the buses at peak hours and placing them at the stops. This reduced the number of conductors required at peak hours and enabled them to collect fares as people waited for buses. Furthermore, conductors were always at the rear entrance, from which they could signal the driver when the bus was ready to move on. At off-peak hours, when there were fewer buses in operation than the number of stops, conductors returned to the buses. The problem was dissolved; *it could not arise in the redesigned system.*

Problems and Disciplines

One of the greatest disservices of formal education lies in the fact that students are made to believe—because of the way courses and curricula are organized—that every problem can be placed in a disciplinary category, such as physical, chemical, biological, psychological, sociological, political, ethical, and so on. However, *there is no such thing as a disciplinary problem.* The world is not organized the way schools, universities, curricula, and courses are, by disciplines. The disciplinary category into which a problem is placed reveals nothing about the nature of the problem, but it may reveal something about the nature of the person who placed it there. Consider the following fable, a story that may not be precisely true but ought to be.

> The production manager of a large paper company had what he saw as a production-scheduling problem. He had a large number of different papers to produce over a relatively small number of production lines. Therefore he frequently had to change production lines from making one product to another. Because of the addition of new papers to the product line and the aging of many old products, there were an increasing number of orders for low-volume products. As a result, there was an increasing number of changeovers (setups) on the production lines, and they consumed an increasing amount of potential production time. Therefore the amount of time spent in production was decreasing and the overheaded unit cost of production was increasing. The manager wanted to find a way of scheduling production so the total setup time was minimized and production costs would be reduced.
>
> The manager's calculations revealed that with a perfect forecast a substantial reduction in production costs could be obtained, but he also found that with the quality of forecasting available to him, the improvement he could actually obtain hardly justified the effort. This appeared to reduce the problem to one of improving forecasting of future demand.
>
> A marketing manager, looking at what the production manager was trying to do, found that about 10 percent of the products accounted for about 90 percent of the sales and a still higher percentage of corporate profits. Many of the low-volume prod-

ucts were sold at a loss. The marketing manager then prepared a list of all the company's products, from the least to the most profitable. Once it was completed, he turned to this question: If the company drops products from its production line starting with the least profitable and working its way up toward the most profitable, how many products would the company have to drop before it could with current practices and procedures obtain a reduction in production costs equal to the theoretical maximum revealed by the previous analysis? The answer surprised him: fewer than 5 percent.

Therefore he proposed an appropriate reduction of the product line to the sales manager. The sales manager pointed out that the least profitable products were purchased by the company's largest and most profitable customers, and therefore he was not willing to experiment with product-line reductions.

When exposed to the marketing manager's effort, a corporate planner with a background in human resources recalled that the company's salesmen were paid a fixed salary plus a commission based on the dollar value of their sales. This meant they earned as much for selling a dollar's worth of unprofitable product as for selling the same amount of profitable product. Therefore he suggested a new compensation system for the salesmen that (1) would pay a commission proportional to the profitability of a sale and pay nothing for unprofitable sales; and (2) the commission rates would be set so that if they had been in effect for the past five years and this had had no effect on what the salesmen sold, their annual earnings would have been the same. On the other hand, if they had sold more of the profitable products, they would have earned more.

The company's executive office agreed to a trial of this compensation system. The results exceeded everyone's expectations. Sales of profitable products increased substantially, and most of the unprofitable products were not sold at all. The salesmen earned more, and company profits increased significantly. The improvement in production that resulted from a reduction of the number of products sold was several times as great as could have been obtained with perfect scheduling and perfect forecasting.

It is important for managers to know that the best place to treat a problem is not necessarily where it appears. For example, a severe production problem caused by the seasonality of sales of a company's principal product was dissolved by adding a product that required the same technology of production but the demand for which ran counter to that of the other. The fluctuation of demand for bathing suits can be countered by producing sweaters for use in cold weather.

Problems should be viewed from as many different perspectives as possible before a way of treating them is selected. Unfortunately, business schools are organized around business functions—for example, finance, accounting, manufacturing, and marketing. Each function defines a business discipline. Consequently, business school courses are organized around business functions or disciplines. Such courses impose on students the belief that every problem falls in one and only one discipline; therefore, other disciplines have nothing constructive to contribute. Business school programs would be much improved if they were organized around sets of interacting problems rather than functions or disciplines. This would enable them to bring multiple points of view to bear on problems, and it would teach students that the categories into which managerial problems are ordinarily placed are quite arbitrary. Furthermore, since the problems confronting management change with changes in the environment, organization of learning around current problems would keep business education dynamic and relevant. Emphasis would be placed on methods of dealing with problems rather than solutions, most of which become obsolete in a relatively short time in a rapidly changing environment.

Problems and Messes

Perhaps the most damaging problem-related misconception derived from the educational process is that problems are objects of experience. They are not. *Problems are abstractions extracted from experience by analysis.* They are related to experience as atoms are to tables. Tables are experienced, not atoms. Managers are not confronted with separate problems but with situations that consist of complex *systems* of strongly interacting problems. I call such situations *messes*.

To understand the damage that derives from assuming problems are objects of direct experience, it is necessary to recall (from Chapter 1) that a system is a whole whose performance depends more on how its parts interact than on how they act when considered separately. The behavior of a system—and a mess is a system—depends more on how its parts interact than on how they act independently of each other. Therefore the effectiveness with which a mess is treated depends on how the treatments of the problems that make it up interact, not on how they act independently of each other. However, students are taught to reduce messes to aggregations of problems, prioritize them, and treat them separately. They are not taught, and do not learn, how to deal effectively with messes taken as a whole.

Business enterprises are also systems. Unfortunately, however, with encouragement from their teachers, business students come to believe that a system's performance can be improved by improving the performance of each of its parts taken separately. This is seldom the case, because parts that are considered to be well managed when considered separately seldom fit together well. Put another way: Business schools teach students how to manage parts of a system efficiently, but effective management focuses on the interactions of parts, the behavior of wholes. An effective marketing manager, for example, is not necessarily one who manages marketing activities well, but one who can coordinate marketing actions with those of other functions and who can induce those in all the other functions to take into account the marketing consequences of what they do.

Business schools act as though understanding the behavior or properties of the parts of a system can be assembled into understanding of the behavior or properties of the whole. Put another way: They act as though analyzing a system can yield understanding of it. The educational system in general and business schools in particular treat analysis and thought as synonyms, but analysis is only one way of thinking. Its product is not understanding but *knowledge* of systems, how their parts act and interact, how they work, their structure. Synthetic thinking is required to gain *understanding* of systems. Understanding comes from determining how they function in the larger systems of which they are part. For example, no amount of taking automobiles apart will reveal why most of them, until recently, were designed to accommodate 6 people. The explanation lies in the fact that they were intended for the average family of the time, which contained 5.6 people. Automobiles are getting smaller today because, among other reasons, the average size of the family has been shrinking. Or, to take another example, explanations for accounting practices cannot be found within accounting but in the role accounting plays in management and the preparation of tax returns.

The deficiencies of business education cannot be removed by changing only what it teaches—that is, its messages. Changes in how it tries to teach are required—that is, its media. What is required is a fundamental redesign of the structure of the educational system and the processes in which it engages. I suggest such a redesign here.

An Idealized Design of a Business School

In this design, I assume the business school is part of a university, but I consider the design of a university only insofar as it affects the design of the business school. *This design incorporates all the ideas presented in the preceding chapters and hence is an exemplification of them.*

I. Financial Structure

The business school would be a profit center in (what would preferably be) a for-profit university. The school or university would include a not-for-profit corporate foundation that could receive research grants and tax-free gifts and endowments. (The internal economy of the school is described below.)

[*It has always struck me as odd that business schools, institutions allegedly devoted to disseminating the virtues of capitalism and the free market system, are organized and operated exactly as institutions are in a centrally planned and controlled economy. This belies the free-enterprise messages they deliver to students.*]

II. Academic Programs

The school would offer only *graduate* degrees in business and management. Although it would not offer an undergraduate degree or major, it would provide introductory and orientation courses for undergraduates. It would also certify levels of competence less than those obtained by completion of a degree.

III. Pedagogy

[*Oscar Wilde wrote: "Education is an admirable thing, but it is well to remember from time to time that nothing that is worth knowing can be taught."*

We cannot predict accurately how many of each type of college graduate that society will need a decade from now. Even if we could, we would still have the problem of allocating fulfillment of these requirements among individual autonomous institutions. Our ability to forecast manpower requirements is not likely to improve because the rate of technological change will continue to increase. This will augment an already considerable tendency of college graduates to switch fields after completing their formal education. For example, W. G. Ireson (1959) reported that surveys over a period of thirty years revealed "that more than 60 percent of those persons who earned (engineering) degrees in the United States, either became managers of some kind within ten to fifteen years or left the engineering profession entirely to enter various kinds of business ventures. . . ." [p. 507]

Even when graduates remain in the field in which they were educated, they have to replace a major portion of their college-acquired knowledge and add to it if they are to maintain their effectiveness. For these reasons, it is essential that college graduates be ready, willing, and able to learn continually.

Because of the increasingly rapid obsolescence of what is learned in school and the increasing tendency to switch fields after graduation, what is learned in school is not nearly as important as their learning how to learn and being motivated to learn continuously.

Learning, learning how to learn, and being motivated to learn continuously can be accomplished in a number of ways, no one the most effective for every student and every subject. However, most of them are more effective than being taught in a conventional classroom. Here are some of them.]

A. Learning Cells

[The best way for a student to learn a well-defined and recorded body of knowledge is to teach it to another. This is common knowledge among those who have taught. Given a number of students each of whom should learn a subject, each cannot teach all of it to all the others. Therefore:]

1. Small groups of students (no more than ten) would be self-organized into learning cells in which they would share responsibility for teaching each other parts of the subject being "taken."

2. Unless asked by the students not to do so, faculty adviser or advisers would attend learning cells and be available as resources to be used by the students as they see fit. Before the beginning of the cell, the adviser or advisers would specify the

minimal subject matter that should be covered, and identify the principal sources that could be used to get into the subject.

3. Students would be evaluated at the end of each cell by the other members of the cell, including faculty, on how much they taught others rather than how much they learned.

[*A subject that has not been well learned cannot be well taught.*]

B. Seminars

Advanced subjects—ones that are either not well developed, well defined, or systematically recorded—would be made available to students through seminars led by faculty members who have demonstrably contributed to the development of the subjects.

1. Such seminars would be concerned at least as much with questions as answers, and as much with developing the underdeveloped subject as reviewing what development there has been. The focus of seminars would be on understanding (explanations)—not knowledge (instruction), or information (description).

2. Students would be evaluated at the end of seminars by the other members of the seminar, including faculty, on how much they have contributed to the development of the subject of the seminar and others' understanding of it.

C. Research Cells

[*Students are motivated to learn and best learn how to do so in solving real problems under real conditions with the guidance of one already so motivated and who knows how to learn. They would do so in research cells.*]

Research cells would consist of no more than ten students working with one or more faculty members on a real system of problems (a mess) in the environment in which the mess exists and, where possible, with the participation of those responsible for doing something about it. Where possible, those responsible for doing something about the mess should pay for the research.

[*This will assure their commitment to the research and the realism of the mess attacked.*]

Students in research cells would be evaluated for their contribution to the dissolution of the mess dealt with. They would be evaluated by each other member of the cell, including faculty, and those responsible for doing something about the mess dealt with.

D. Instructional Courses

These would include studios and laboratories and would be used to develop skills—for example, surveying, drafting, and speaking a foreign language. Faculty would evaluate students in these courses for their ability to apply the skills they have learned in the real world.

E. Independent Study

Students could elect this as a way to learn any subject on their own. Those who elect independent study would be evaluated by the faculty member or members under whose supervision the students would do their work.

F. Lectures

Each year, each member of the faculty would give a series of lectures that students could attend but without credit. These lectures would be videotaped and be made available in subsequent years through the university's library. Videotapes of similar series presented by outstanding faculty of other institutions would also be obtained and made available to students and faculty. Copies of the tapes of lectures made at this school would be made available to others for purchase or rent.

IV. Evaluation of Students

[*Note that conventional examinations—questions to be answered or exercises to be solved—would not be used to evaluate students in any of the learning situations described. This would eliminate cheating. Cheating is more an evil of the conventional examination system than of students. Typical closed-book examinations are not an adequate model of any real situation in which a person must demonstrate his competence in a subject.*

Note also that the type of pedagogy and examinations described requires large amounts of personal interactions between students and faculty members.]

    A. Faculty members would meet at the end of each term to formulate a collective evaluation of the performance of each student. These evaluations would be reviewed with students by their advisers and placed in their record and would focus on ways the students could improve rather than on what they had done wrong.

    B. The faculty might advise students whose work and prospects are unsatisfactory to leave the program. Nevertheless, the students could elect to continue. If their work remained unsatisfactory, the faculty could drop them.

V. Admission to a Program

    A. There would be no entry requirements to the school, only exit requirements. However, each applicant would be evaluated by a faculty-student committee—three of each—to determine whether in their opinion the student is suitable. Whenever possible, applicants would be interviewed by at least one member of the committee or a graduate of the program who is more accessible to the applicants. If applicants were found to be unsuitable, they would be so advised, but they would still be free to enter the school.

[*Experience with such an arrangement has shown that students would be very unlikely to do so when made aware of stringent exit requirements. After all, they are not motivated to waste their time and money.*]

   B. The student who entered the school despite advice to the contrary should not be identified to any member of the faculty, administrative staff, or student body. Any member of the evaluating committee who did so would be suspended from the school for one year.

VI. Curricula

   A. No courses would be required. However, there would be a list of subjects that entering students would be expected to know before they leave the school. Successful completion of a cell, course, seminar, or independent study devoted to one of these subjects would be taken as fulfillment of that requirement. For those subjects not so covered, oral examinations would be given. These would take the form of a discussion with no less than three members of the faculty, at least one of whom is selected by the student involved.
   B. Masters and doctoral degrees would be offered.
   C. Preparation of an acceptable thesis would be required for each graduate degree. The thesis for a Ph.D. would be expected to contribute to the development of the field. The thesis for the D.S. would be expected to be an innovative application of what is already known to a real situation.

[The Ph.D. would be the more suitable degree for those who intend to enter an academic or research career; the D.S., for those who intend to practice in nonacademic organizations.]

   D. Students would be able to take a suggested program or design one of their own.
      1. The faculty would make available descriptions of programs of study that students could follow as is, or modify as they saw fit. Their modifications would have to be approved by a faculty committee.

2. Students could design their own programs of study and submit them to faculty committees of three, with whom they would be discussed. Programs of study might include any cells and courses given in the university and, with faculty approval, courses given at other institutions. They might also include seminars, independent study, and applied work, particularly apprenticeships. If a proposed course of study were found to be suitable, the student would be authorized to follow that program. Subsequent changes would be permitted with the approval of the student's adviser.

E. Each student would either select an adviser (who would have to agree to serve in this capacity) or have one assigned. Later, each student would select a thesis adviser (who would have the right of refusal) or have one assigned.

F. Theses would be required.

1. Oral thesis examinations would be conducted by committees of five, which would include no more than three members of the faculty drawn from the relevant program. Two or more examiners would be drawn from other programs or from outside the university. The student would have the right to select two of the examiners and to invite as many as three other students to attend the examination.

2. A thesis could either be (a) accepted as submitted, (b) accepted subject to revisions to be reviewed by one or more designated faculty members, or (c) rejected. Those whose theses were rejected would be given a second, but no further, chance to redo and resubmit it.

VII. Continuing Education

A. The school would provide a wide variety of continuing education programs, varying in length from several days to several years. These would yield certificates or, in some cases, degrees.

B. The school would also provide competence maintenance programs that, for a fixed annual fee, would keep their subscribers up to date in one or more fields they select. They would receive annual reviews that inform them of significant developments made in the past year in these fields. In addition, subscribers would be given an opportunity to come to the school for discussion of these reviews with the faculty and students who prepared them and with each other.

VIII. Research and Practice

A. All full-time faculty members would spend at least half of their time on research or in practice that involved at least three students.

B. The research and practice engaged in would be administered and managed through one or more research centers, institutes, or groups that are part of the school.

C. At least half of the practice engaged in through the centers would be at the frontier of the field involved and therefore require research.

D. Research and practice would be billed to clients on a cost-plus basis. Costs would include salaries and benefits provided to faculty and students. Where the client is a for-profit organization, the "plus" would be large enough to enable the center to accumulate funds that could be used for development.

E. Students would be compensated for their work on projects but faculty would not—it would be considered part of their job. However, faculty would be permitted to spend up to three days per month on personal consulting or other activities that contribute to their personal development.

F. All students would either be (1) employed up to half time on center-based projects, (2) engaged on such projects without compensation, or (3) employed outside the university doing work that is related to their programs of study. The relevance of their work to their programs would be judged by their advisers.

IX. Publications

A. The school would operate a press for publication of books, monographs, journals, and audio- and audiovisual tapes.

B. The press would operate as a profit center.

X. Organization

The school would have a multidimensional organization, with input, output, and executive units.

A. *Input units* would be units whose output (products or services) would be consumed primarily by people within the school. These units would be of three types: academic departments, libraries, and service units.

1. Departments would be defined by a common competence—skill or interest. Every faculty member would be a member of at least one department. Faculty members who belong to more than one department would designate one of them as their principal affiliation.

   a. Departments would have responsibility for all faculty personnel transactions and for their continuous development.

   b. The only income that departments would receive would come from sale of their members' time to other units inside or outside the school. Departments would set prices on their faculty members' time.

   c. Departments would be profit centers. They would be able to retain a specified portion of their profits for their discretionary use.

2. The school's library would provide a complete array of documents, publications, and tapes together with equipment for their use and reproduction. Through interlibrary loans it would provide access to other libraries, and

through computer networks would also provide access to all relevant external information sources.

   a. The library would be a cost center supported by the executive office of the school.

3. Service units in the school, or the university that contains the school, would carry out such functions as finance, admissions, placement, financial aid, records, registration, audiovisual, duplicating, bookstore, housing, dining, purchasing, buildings and grounds, human resources, health, and mail.

   a. Some service units would operate as profit centers, selling their services to other units at prices they establish. They would also be free to sell their services externally, subject to an executive override to be discussed below. Those service units that operate exclusively within the school (e.g., admissions, registrar, and mail) would operate as cost centers supported by the school's executive office.

   b. All units would be free to provide themselves with the services they require, or to buy them from either internal or external service units, subject to executive override.

B. *Output units* provide products or services that are primarily consumed by external consumers. They would be of three types: academic programs, research centers (institutes or groups), and the press.

1. Each academic program and research center would have a faculty that does not contain a majority of its members from any one department or discipline.

[*This is intended to encourage inter- and transdisciplinarity.*]

   a. Faculty members' affiliations with programs and research centers would last only as long as their performance was satisfactory and as long as they and their departments were willing to let them participate in the programs or centers.

b. Each program and center would operate as profit centers, deriving income from tuition, research, and consulting. They would be responsible for providing financial support to students who are part of them.

c. Faculty members participating in research centers would receive no extra compensation for doing so, but their other responsibilities would be reduced.

2. The school's press would publish books, journals, and tapes, and operate as a profit center.

C. The school would have an executive office consisting of a dean and, depending on the size of the school, the following vice deans:

1. A vice dean of academic affairs, to whom the heads of academic programs, the director of the press, the dean of the faculty, and the director of the library would report.

2. A vice dean of research, to whom the directors of all freestanding research centers would report directly, and to whom the directors of research centers incorporated in academic programs would have an indirect reporting relation.

3. A vice dean of services, to whom the directors of all service units would report.

4. The executive office would be a profit center.

a. Its income would derive from (a) a tax imposed on the profits of all units that operate as profit centers and (b) interest charged for capital that it provides for use by these units.

b. Its costs would include the costs of units that it includes and that operate as cost centers, and the costs associated with its overrides of selections of sources of services or supplies by profit centers.

1. If a profit center were required by the executive office to acquire a service from an internal unit when

it could obtain that service less expensively from an external supplier, the executive office would be required to pay that unit the difference in cost.

   2. If the executive office deprived a profit center of the right to sell its services to an external customer, it would have to pay that unit an amount equal to the lost profit.

5. Units and individuals would support the executive function. Depending on what the university provides, they might include external relations (including alumni affairs and recruiting), planning and development, and financial services (e.g., auditing, accounting, and the controller).

XI. Management Style

A. The school would have a circular organization as described in Chapter 4. In addition, all students enrolled in academic programs would participate as members of the boards of these programs on issues that affect them.

[Note that this means that every member of the university, including students, will be on at least the board of his or her immediate superior.]

B. All administrators would have the following functions:

   1. To create an environment and provide support that enhances the effectiveness of all who are part of the school.

[Subordinates who require supervision are not fit for their jobs. Work of those who are fit requires facilitation, not supervision.]

   2. To manage the interactions of their units with other units in the university. Administrators would focus on managing over and up, not down.

   3. To control allocation of resources as specified in unit plans to units subordinate to them.

   4. To define the minimal responsibilities and authority of

their subordinates. As little job-specifying should be done as possible, thereby allowing individuals to do as much as they feel qualified to do.

5. To encourage and facilitate the development of their subordinates.

6. To manage those subordinates who are themselves administrators "by objectives." Objectives would be set in negotiation with immediate superiors. Once set, subordinates would be free to select whatever means they want.

XII. Faculty

A. All faculty members would have the same rank and title: professor.

B. Tenure would not be provided to faculty members (because it protects incompetence more than it protects academic freedom, and there are more effective ways of protecting academic freedom). The initial appointments of those who have had no previous academic experience would be for two years. Subsequent appointments would be for four years, eight years, sixteen years, and until retirement. Initial appointments for those with previous academic experience would take such experience into account.

[*For example, a person who has been in academia for ten years would receive an eight-year appointment. Those with twenty years, a sixteen-year appointment, and so on.*]

C. Academic freedom would be protected. A board of five members of other academic institutions, each appointed for five-year renewable and staggered terms, would hear any appeals concerning violation of such freedom. Its decision will be final. Members of this board must have the approval of a majority of the standing faculty members.

D. Faculty members would be profit centers. Their income would consist of a designated amount for each student credit hour they provide and the payment their department receives for their time spent on research. Faculty members who incur annual losses would receive no increase in salary for the following year. Those who incurred losses in two consecutive years would not be reappointed unless they received executive approval when their contracts ran out.

E. Faculty members' salaries would consist of a fixed component and a variable component. The variable component would take into account their profitability, the amount of research they have brought to the school or university, and the amount and quality of their publications, all in the past year. The fixed part of their salaries would be approximately 75 percent of their market value.

F. Faculty members would be evaluated annually by (1) the students who have worked with them that year, (2) their peers in their departments and in the programs and research centers in which they have participated that year, and (3) the heads of these departments, programs, and research centers. These evaluations would be reviewed with faculty members by their departmental chairpersons each year, then made a matter of record and used in setting their salary levels and deciding whether to renew their contracts.

G. Faculty salaries would be set by the chairperson of their departments.

H. Renewal of a contract would require approval by a majority of the members of a faculty member's department.

XIII. Academic Schedule

A. The academic year would be divided into trimesters, each fifteen weeks long. There would be two two-week breaks and one three-week break between trimesters.

B. Each student not employed on a continuing basis by a research center or as a learning assistant would study during two trimesters and engage in relevant work for the third (Fig. E.1).

Trimester

Year	1	2	3
1	Study	Study	Work
2	Study	Work	Study
3	Work	Study	Study

Fig. E.1. An idealized schedule for a business school.

[*This schedule would enable research centers and other external as well as internal employers of students to have a workforce of constant size throughout the year. It would also enable more senior students to orient and instruct those who are more junior on the work to be done. Finally, it would reduce facility requirements because the entire student body would never be in session at the same time.*]

XIV. Facilities

    A. Every faculty member would have a private office with sufficient room to hold at least three visitors at a time.

    B. Every student would be provided with a desk, a bookcase, and a file cabinet.

    C. A sufficient number of personal computers would be provided so that each faculty member and student either has, or has easy access to, one. A comprehensive integrated network would tie together a central computing facility, the libraries, research centers, program and departmental units, service units, and individual PCs.

D. All the usual service facilities associated with a university or school would also be provided—for example, housing, dining, recreational facilities, a school store, and so on.

E. If the university or school were located in a climate in which inclement weather is not unusual, all buildings would be connected by enclosed walkways.

Conclusion

Education has long been considered to be an important investment in the future. Today, however, it would be accurate to consider business-school education as an investment in the past. To a very large extent such education is occupied with transmitting those outdated concepts, principles, and practices that are responsible for the decline of the economy of the United States.

Universities have increasingly forsaken their traditional role of constructive critic of society. It was their function to confront society with the truth about itself. They served as both the memory and the conscience of society. They provided the one place from which one could freely criticize society and propose radical changes in it without fear of recrimination. Academic tenure was created to assure this freedom of academics to criticize and propose. Today, however, the principal function of tenure is to protect the jobs of the incompetent.

The growing financial dependence of both private and public institutions of higher learning on government funding has taken its toll. Academics are acutely aware of the principal source of the butter on their bread and, in the case of public institutions, of the bread itself. Academics are not inclined to bite the hand that feeds them, and that hand is attached to a mind that wants its behavior rationalized, not criticized.

Corporations are another major source of support for institutions of higher learning. In general, however, the executives who make the decisions about how much to give and to whom expect no criticism of their management from business schools in return. They have no intention of supporting threats to their security, standard of living, and status in society. They want graduates with knowledge that will enable them to pursue their objectives more efficiently but without radical change, and they want no questions raised about the legitimacy of their objectives. Because this desire is not being satisfied to the extent corporate executives would like, they are increasingly supplying their own business education:

> Educational programs run by business and industry have become a "booming industry" that now constitutes an alternative, if not a threat, to traditional colleges and universities, according to the Carnegie Foundation for the Advancement of Teaching. . . .
>
> The 240-page study "Corporate Classrooms: The Learning Business," reported that at least 18 corporations and industry wide associations now award academic degrees that are or soon will be recognized by regional accrediting agencies, and 8 more have plans to do so by 1988. [Fiske, 1985 p. A10]

Foundations, a third major source of support for business schools, tend to be in the service of governments and corporations. They are not dedicated to shaking any boats. They seldom support efforts to produce fundamental change.

Terrel H. Bell, former U.S. secretary of education, is reported to have said, "We cannot truly reform U.S. education until its failures become a national obsession" (*Business Week*, December 10, 1990, p. 10ED). Business can't afford to wait. From where will the leadership required to make the failure of business education a business obsession come?

Appendix
Thinking Backward

The following example illustrates the fact that a problem in which the destination or endpoint is known can usually be solved more easily by working backward from the destination to the origin rather than from the origin to the destination. For example, mazes are usually easier to solve by working from the exit to the entrance than from the entrance to the exit. One need not follow the algebra in detail to get the point of the following example.

A farmer went to market with a basket of apples. He met a friend and gave him half his apples plus half an apple. Later, he met a second friend and gave him half his remaining apples plus half an apple. He did the same for a third friend and a fourth. After his fourth friend he had no apples left. How many did he start with?

First let's try to solve this problem working from the beginning to the end. The farmer started off with x apples and gave $(\frac{1}{2}x + \frac{1}{2})$ apples, to his first friend. This left him with $x - (\frac{1}{2}x + \frac{1}{2})$ apples when he approached his second friend. Therefore, he gave his second friend $\frac{1}{2}[x - (\frac{1}{2}x + \frac{1}{2})] + \frac{1}{2}$ apples, leaving him with $x - (\frac{1}{2}x + \frac{1}{2}) - \{\frac{1}{2}[x - (\frac{1}{2}x + \frac{1}{2})] + \frac{1}{2}\}$ apples. He then gave half this quantity plus half an apple to his third friend: $\frac{1}{2}((x - \frac{1}{2}x + \frac{1}{2}) - \{\frac{1}{2}[x - (\frac{1}{2}x + \frac{1}{2})] + \frac{1}{2}\} + \frac{1}{2}))$. This left him with $x - (\frac{1}{2}x + \frac{1}{2}) - \{\frac{1}{2}[x - (\frac{1}{2}x + \frac{1}{2})] + \frac{1}{2}\} - ((\frac{1}{2}[x - (\frac{1}{2}x + \frac{1}{2}) - \{\frac{1}{2}[x - (\frac{1}{2}x + \frac{1}{2}) + \frac{1}{2}\}$

$+ \frac{1}{2}))$. Finally he gave his last friend: $\frac{1}{2} [[x - (\frac{1}{2} x + \frac{1}{2}) - \{\frac{1}{2} [x - (\frac{1}{2}x + \frac{1}{2})] + \frac{1}{2}\} - ((\frac{1}{2} [x - (\frac{1}{2}x + \frac{1}{2}) - \{\frac{1}{2} [x - (\frac{1}{2} x + \frac{1}{2}) + \frac{1}{2}\} + \frac{1}{2}))]] + \frac{1}{2}$. The amount then left after his fourth friend was: $x - (\frac{1}{2} x + \frac{1}{2}) - \{\frac{1}{2} [x - (\frac{1}{2} x + \frac{1}{2})] + \frac{1}{2}\} - [[\frac{1}{2} ((x - (\frac{1}{2} x + \frac{1}{2}) - \{\frac{1}{2} [x - (\frac{1}{2} x + \frac{1}{2})] + \frac{1}{2})) + \frac{1}{2}]] - \{\{x - (\frac{1}{2}x + \frac{1}{2}) - \{\frac{1}{2} [x - (\frac{1}{2}x + \frac{1}{2})] + \frac{1}{2}\} - [[\frac{1}{2} ((x - (\frac{1}{2} x + \frac{1}{2}) - \{\frac{1}{2} [x - (\frac{1}{2}x + \frac{1}{2})] + \frac{1}{2})) + \frac{1}{2}]]\}\}$. This last quantity must be set equal to zero and solved. This is not a difficult process but it is a very long and tedious task.

Now, let's start at the end and work backward. The farmer had x apples left when he reached his last friend and gave him $\frac{1}{2} x + \frac{1}{2}$ apples which, when subtracted from x, is equal to zero: $x - (\frac{1}{2} x + \frac{1}{2}) = 0$. Solving this, $x = 1$. Continuing to work backward arithmetically, the farmer could not have had 2 apples when he reached his third friend because when $\frac{1}{2} (2) + \frac{1}{2}$ is subtracted from 2 the result is not 1, which he had left after leaving his third friend. It seems natural then to try 3. This works because $3 - [\frac{1}{2} (3) + \frac{1}{2}] = 3 - 2 = 1$. Then the farmer could not have had 6 or less when he reached his second friend because $6 - [\frac{1}{2} (6) + \frac{1}{2}] = 6 - 3\frac{1}{2} = 3$, but $7 - [\frac{1}{2} (7) + \frac{1}{2}] = 7 - 4 = 3$. The principle is now clear: multiply the last number by 2 and add 1. Therefore, he began with $2 (7) + 1 = 15$.

It takes only a minute or two to solve this problem backward and as much as an hour to do it forward. The simplification that results from working backward is apparent. The number we started with when working backward could only take on one value: 1. However, when we worked forward the number we started with could take on the value of any positive integer of which there are an infinite number. The difference between 1 and infinity (∞) is very large.

References

Ackoff, Russell L. *Creating the Corporate Future*. New York: John Wiley & Sons, 1981.

————. "The Resurrection of A&P" in *Management in Small Doses*." New York: John Wiley & Sons, 1986, pp. 53–56.

————. "The Circular Organization: An Update," *The Academy of Management* 3/1 (February 1989): 11–16.

———— and William B. Deane. "The Revitalization of ALCOA's Tennessee Operations," *National Productivity Review* (Summer 1984): 239–45.

———— and Francisco Sagasti. "Possible and Likely Futures in Urban Transportation," *Socio-Economic Planning Science* 5 (1971): 413–28.

———— and Elsa Vergara. "Creativity in Problem-Solving and Planning: A Review." *European Journal of Operational Research* 7 (1981): 1–13.

Ansoff, H. Igor. *Corporate Strategy*. New York: McGraw-Hill Book Company, 1965.

Arthur D. Little, "Companies Continue to Embrace Quality Programs, but TQM Has Generated More Enthusiasm Than Results," press release (March 1992).

Bartol, Julio R., and Ali Geranmayeh. "Corporate Integrity and Internal Market Economies" in Halal et al. (1993).

Beer, Stafford. *The Brain of the Firm*. London: Allen Lane, The Penguin Press, 1972.

————. *The Heart of the Enterprise*. Chichester, Eng.: John Wiley & Sons, 1979.

Bellman, Richard. "On the Theory of Programming," *Proceedings of the National Academy of Sciences of the United States of America*. 38/8 (August 15, 1952): 716–19.

Bennett, Amanda. "Making the Grade with the Customer," *The Wall Street Journal* (November 12, 1990), p. B1f.

Bierce, Ambrose. *The Enlarged Devil's Dictionary*. Harmondsworth, Eng.: Penguin Books, 1967.

Blumberg, Paul. *Industrial Democracy*. New York: Schocken Books, 1969.

Burke, W. Warner. *Organizational Development*. Reading, Mass.: Addison-Wesley Publishing Company, 1987.

Burnham, James. *The Managerial Revolution*. New York: The John Day Company, 1941.

Carlzon, Jan. *Moments of Truth*. Cambridge, Mass.: Ballinger Publishing Company, 1987.

Charlton, John. "Creating Customer-Focused R&D: A Plan for Esso Petroleum Canada" in Halal et al. (1993).

Choukroun, Jean-Marc and Roberta M. Snow, eds., *Planning for Human Systems*. Philadelphia: University of Pennsylvania Press, 1992.

Coffey, Wayne. *303 of World's Worst Predictions*. New York: Tribeca Communications, 1983.

Cooper-Hewitt Museum, the Smithsonian Institution's National Museum of Design. *The Phenonenon of Change*. New York, 1984.

Crosby, Philip B., *Quality Is Free: The Art of Making Quality Certain*. New York: McGraw Hill, 1979.

Cyert, R. M., and J. G. March. *A Behavioral Theory of the Firm*. Englewood Cliffs, N.J.: Prentice-Hall, 1963.

Davis, Stanley M., and Paul R. Lawrence. *Matrix*. Reading, Mass.: Addison-Wesley Publishing Company, 1977.

Deming, W. Edwards. *Out of Crisis*. Cambridge, Mass.: MIT Center for Advanced Engineering Study, 1986.

Dewey, John. *Logic: The Theory of Inquiry*. New York: Henry Holt and Company, 1938.

Diebold, John. *Automation: The Advent of the Automatic Factory*. New York: D. Van Nostrand Company, 1952.

Dobyns, Lloyd, and Clare Crawford-Mason. *Quality or Else*. Boston: Houghton Mifflin Company, 1991.

Drucker, Peter F. *The Age of Discontinuity*. New York: Harper & Row, 1968.

———. "Permanent Cost-Cutting," *The Wall Street Journal* (January 11, 1991), p. A10.

Egner, Robert E., ed. *Bertramd Russell's Best*. New York: The New American Library, 1958.

Emery, F. E., and E. L. Trist. "The Causal Texture of Organizational Environments," *Human Relations* 18/1 (February 1965): 21–32.

Emshoff, James R., and Teri E. Demlinger. *The New Rules of the Game*. New York: HarperCollins, 1991.

Evan, William M. *Organization Theory: Research and Design*. New York: Macmillan Publishing Company, 1993.

Feigenbaum, Armand V. "American on the Threshold of Quality," *Quality* (January 1990): pp. 16–18.

Fiske, Edward B. "Booming Corporate Education Efforts Rival College Programs, Study Says," *The New York Times*, (January 28, 1985), p. A10.

Flood, Robert L. *Beyond TQM*. Chichester, Eng.: John Wiley & Sons, 1993.

Fortune. "Now Hear This" (October 27, 1986), p. 14.

Friedman, Milton J. "The Social Responsibility of Business Is to Increase Its Profits," *The New York Times Magazine* (September 13, 1970), p. 32f.

———. "The Voucher Idea," *The New York Times Magazine* (September 23, 1973), p. 23f.

Galbraith, Jay. *Designing Complex Organizations*. Reading, Mass.: Addison-Wesley Publishing Company, 1973.

Gharajedaghi, Jamshid. *Toward a Systems Theory of Organization*. Seaside, Calif.: Intersystems Publications, 1985.

Goggin, William C. "How the Multidimensional Structure Works at Dow Corning," *Harvard Business Review* 52 (January–February 1974): 54–65.

Halal, William, Geranmayeh, and John Pourdehnad, eds., *Internal Markets*. New York: John Wiley & Sons, 1993.

Hamel, Gary, and C. K. Prahalad. "Strategy as Stretch and Leverage," *Harvard Business Review* 71/2 (March–April 1993): 75–84.

Hoerr, John, and Harris Collingwood. "The Battle for Corporate Control," *Business Week* (May 18, 1987): 102–7.

Ireson, W. G., "Preparation for Business in Engineering Schools" in *The Education of American Businessmen*, ed. F. C. Pierson et al. New York: McGraw-Hill, 1959.

Jenks, C. "Giving Money for Schooling: Educational Vouchers," *Phi Delta Kappan* (September 1970): 49–52.

Jennings E. G. "The World of the Executive," *TWA Ambassador* 4 (1971): 28–30.

Jeuck, John E. *Pride and Prejudice,* Tower/Cresap Lecture (1986), Selected Paper No. 64. Chicago: University of Chicago Graduate School of Business (February 1987), pp. 1–24.

Joyce, James. *The Portable James Joyce.* New York: The Viking Press, 1947.

Juran, J. M. *Juran on Leadership for Quality: An Executive Handbook.* New York: The Free Press, 1988.

Knox, Andrea. "Most Cuts in Jobs Don't Help Firms, Survey Indicates," *The Philadelphia Inquirer* (March 9, 1992), p. Dl.

Kuhn, Thomas S. *The Structure of Scientific Revolutions,* 2nd ed. Chicago: The University of Chicago Press, 1970.

Langer, S. K. *Philosophy in a New Key.* New York: Penguin Books, 1948.

Levy, Amir, and Uri Merry. *Organization Transformation: Approaches, Strategies, Theories.* New York: Praeger Publishers, 1986.

Lucky, Robert W. "Reflectlions: What's Goning On?" *IEEE Spectrum* (November 1990): 6.

McCluhan, Marshall. *Understanding Media.* New York: Signet Books, 1964.

Maccoby, Michael. *Why Work.* New York: Simon & Schuster, 1988.

McWhinney, Will. *Paths of Change.* Newbury Park, Calif.: Sage Publications, 1992.

Meadows, Donella H., D. C. Meadows, J. Randers, and W. W. Behrens III. *The Limits to Growth.* New York: Universe Books, 1972.

Miller, G. A. "The Magical Seven, Plus or Minus Two: Some Limits on Our Capacity for Processing Information," *Psychological Review* 63 (1956): 81–97.

Mouzells, N. P. "Bureaucracy," *The New Encylopaedia Britannica.* 15th ed., *Macropaedia* 3 (1974).

Muller, Helen J., James L. Porter, and Robert R. Reader. "Reinventing the MBA the European Way," *Business Horizons* (May/June 1991): 83–91.

Naisbitt, John. *Megatrends.* New York: Warner Books, 1982.

Newman, Edwin. "A Witches' Caldron Called Futurology," *Eastern Review* (October 1980): 28–30.

Ogillvy, James. "This Postmodern Business," *The Deeper News* 1/5 (November 1989): 3–23.

Pfendt, Henry G. "Outsourcing—Strategic Alliances and Partnerships in the Context of New Strategic Realities" in Halal et al. (1993).

Rahman, Md. Aisur. "Towards an Alternative Development Paradigm," *IFDA Dossier* 81 (April/June 1991): 17–27.

Rappaport, Alfred. *Creating Shareholder Value,* New York: The Free Press, 1986.

Rinehart, James R. "The Executive Office Should Also Be a Profit Center" in Halal et al. (1993).

Rosenbluth, Hal F. *The Customer Comes Second.* New York: William Morrow & Company, 1992.

Roth, William F., Jr. *A Systems Approach to Quality Improvement.* New York: Praeger Publishers, 1992.

Saad, Kamal N. "Invention vs. Innovation: Gaps and Bridges," a talk given to the Harvard Club of Belgium, conference "Business Innovation and the Role of the University," Brussels (November 5, 1984).

Samuelson, Robert J. "What Good Are B-Schools?," *Newsweek* (May 14, 1990), p. 49.

Savas, E. S. *Privatizing the Public Sector.* Chatham, N.J.: Chatham House Publishers, 1982.

Schon, Donald A. *Beyond the Stable State.* New York: Random House, 1971.

Scott Morton, Michael S., ed. *The Corporation of the 1990s.* New York: Oxford University Press, 1991.

Shewhart, Walter A. *Statistical Methods from the Viewpoint of Quality Control.* Department of Agriculture, Graduate School, 1939.

Singer, E. A., Jr. *In Search of a Way of Life.* New York: Columbia University Press, 1948.

——. *On the Contented Life.* New York: Henry Holt, 1923.

Stark, Werner. *The Fundamental Forms of Social Thought.* New York: Fordham University Press, 1963.

Starr, John P. "Reintroducing Alcoa to Economic Reality" in Halal et al. (1993).

Taylor, Frederick W. *The Principles of Scientific Management.* New York: Harper & Brothers, 1911.

Tichy, Noel. *Business Horizons* (May 1, 1991).

Toffler, Alvin. *Future Shock.* New York: Bantam Books, 1971.

Townsend, Robert. *Up the Organization.* Greenwich, Conn.: Fawcett Publications, 1970.

Trist, Eric. "The Evolution Socio-Technical Systems," *Issues in the Quality of Working Life* 2 (June 1981), Ontario Ministry of Labor.

———. "Intervention Strategies for Interorganizational Domains" in R. Tannenbaum et al., eds., *Human Systems Development.* San Francisco: Jossey-Bass, 1985.

Valery, Paul. *The Outlook for Intelligence.* Princeton, N.J.: Princeton University Press, 1989.

Work in America: Report of a Special Task Force to the Secretary of Health, Education, and Welfare. Cambridge, Mass.: The MIT Press, 1973.

Zeleny, Milan, ed. *Autopoiesis: A Theory of Living Organization.* New York: North Holland, 1991.

Suggested Readings

Ackoff, Russell, L. *Creating the Corporate Future.* New York: John Wiley & Sons, 1981.

Checkland, Peter. *Systems Thinking, Systems Practice.* Chichester, Eng.: John Wiley & Sons, 1981.

Churchman, C. West. *The Systems Approach and Its Enemies.* New York: Basic Books, 1979.

Emery, F. E., ed. *Systems Thinking,* vols. 1 and 2. Penguin Books, Harmondsworth, Middlesex, Eng.: Penguin Books, 1981.

Flood, Robert L., and Michael C. Jackson. *Creative Problem-Solving.* Chichester, Eng., John Wiley & Sons, 1991.

Kauffman, Draper L., Jr. *Systems 1: An Introduction to Systems Thinking.* Minneapolis: Future Systems, 1980.

Senge, Peter M. *The Fifth Discipline.* New York: Doubleday, 1990.

Index